a beautiful healing

JENNIFER OSBORN

praise for a beautiful healing

"In *A Beautiful Healing* Jennifer Osborn courageously shares her story, simultaneously inviting you to witness the depths of heartbreak that comes from childhood trauma, and the incredible healing that is available to you no matter what you've gone through. I cannot recommend this book more highly! It will give you lenses to see with eyes of hope, and enlarge your belief that God can bring about a beautiful healing in even the worst of circumstances."
-**CHUCK MINGO** – PASTOR

"God has a way of bringing A Beautiful Healing into the most broken heart. This is a raw, true story of how God captured the heart of a troubled girl and brought A Beautiful Healing into her life. I was rocked by reading Jennifer Osborn's account of her upbringing. Abused, abandoned, suicidal, and lost--but Jesus won her heart. This is the redemption story of a lost lamb who has become a devoted lover of God. I was gripped by the raw intensity of Jennifer's life story. It will move your heart and convince you that nothing and no one is beyond the reach of the merciful hands of Almighty God. I promise you; this is a book that can impact your life for years to come! Read it! And buy a copy for a friend, they will thank you for it!"

-Dr. Brian Simmons, Passion & Fire Ministries, The Passion Translation Project

"*A Beautiful Healing* is a poignant memoir of childhood tragedy, and how God's unwavering love is more powerful than any past trauma or shame. Jennifer's story will break your heart and put it back together, proving that hope is just on the other side of forgiveness."

– Lorie Langdon, Young adult author

"The way Jennifer wrote her story you will feel like you are sitting in the room with her. Be ready to journey back in time with Jen as she takes a good, hard look at her life. You will be blown away at all the things she uncovers and heals along the way. This is a must-read book for anyone who has ever felt like giving up. Jennifer's story will help you keep the faith and hope alive in your own life. The Lord has brought such A Beautiful Healing into Jen's life and as her friend it has been beautiful to see her continue to grow."

-Tiffany Brearton, Author of From Stilettos to Grace

"Jesus teaches us through the gospels the importance of storytelling and how stories can penetrate hearts and reveal possibilities that are outside of our understanding. Isn't it true that stories can often speak loudest? Isn't it true that stories inspire and stir the hearts of those who hear them? Jennifer captures this art of inspiration in her book through the riveting details of her life's testimony. You will be filled with hope and reminded of how big God is as you journey with her through this book. If you have ever questioned how far God's arm will reach, then this book is for you. If you have ever wondered how big His plan is, then this book is for you."

LISA SCHWARZ, C.B.C. C.P.C. B.H.C., FOUNDER, CEO OF CRAZY8 MINISTRIES

❀

"My experience with this book was an amazing one. I recommend this book to people going on a journey to understand the 'why,' the 'what', and sometimes even 'where' of self-discovery. I've come to understand by reading this book that sometimes there aren't any answers, just good-byes and letting go of what you wanted - jumping and falling into what is and waiting for what will become.

Jennifer's journey began at an early age, experiencing some traumatic things that happened to her and things that were also missing in her life. I like to compliment her on exposing and sharing those wounded places in her life and being willing to say to other people that even when you're wounded and don't understand it if you wait long enough, the answer will come.

As I was reading the beginning and her middle journey, the end struck me as a way for someone to realize that healing doesn't always come all at once, but if you wait on it, it will come. I've known Jennifer for three years, and I've grown to love her dearly. She is an example of how people become different things for different reasons. Jennifer is a wholehearted servant. Despite her woundedness, Jennifer has learned to love and like people deeply. I've watched her in many venues as a servant, and after reading her book, it lets me understand why that is.

I recommend this book to anyone on a journey of discovering what healing is and how beautiful it can be. As we heal, we're also walking towards being whole, and that's what Jennifer is doing.

- **LUCRETIA BOWMAN,** VICE PRESIDENT OF RECOVERY SERVICES, CITY GOSPEL MISSION

❀

"I knew bits and pieces of Jennifer's story, but to read it in black and white blew me away. Strong, powerful, events and emotions, leading to an amazing redemption. Jen's story will touch your heart, but also remind you how strong a woman of God can truly be."

-**STACY MANGAN**

To Lindsay and Sarah.

And to you, who quietly sit in the dark, believing the lies your false guilt tells you. You can step out into the light and learn the truth of who you really are.

disclaimer

Some names were changed and people omitted to protect identities. Whenever possible, events were kept as they occurred.

In the following pages I speak of trauma that happened to me. I want you to be aware of this, and hope you are not triggered by anything you read. I strove to keep the descriptions undamaging while at the same time preserving the truth.

introduction

Memories are like water. Fluid, drifting, taking on different shapes depending on what obstacle they hit. Mine are like that. Events shaped me to an extent but didn't define me. They are the narrative of my experience—of how I processed abuse, turmoil, and chaos. They are interpreted differently by everyone who lived them.

This story is my truth, my emotions, my pain as I felt it.

I've been asked many times why I want to tell my story, and that question always surprises me. Why wouldn't I want to tell my story? I realize what I'm sharing may cause a visceral response to the immense pain and extreme situations I experienced. But even in the midst of my story, there's an underlying rock that doesn't move.

God.

While I didn't realize it at the time, He was right there with me in my pain, and is the author of my continued healing. He is my hope and the only reason I continue to breathe. He was there on the dark nights when I considered taking my own life, and was what saved me when I turned those thoughts to actions. His hands held me close when my parents did not. He is the truth that fought off the lies I believed about myself.

God is the purpose for my telling this story. Without him, my story is just words on a sheet of paper. Without his presence I'd be dead emotionally. So, I pray that by the end of reading this book, you see God's hand on my life and his divine providence in each drop of hope in what seems like a hopeless situation. He is why I'm here—and why you're here too. He can move in your life and heal you just like he did me. Even if the world says you are the child of a monster, I hope you realize you are the child of a King.

With love,

Jen

the arrest

The moment my life completely unraveled was the same moment I started walking toward restoration. I didn't realize it at the time, but the worst thing that could happen also forged the path that set me free.

The abrupt end of life with my dad came on a warm May afternoon. My sophomore-year finals were about to begin and summer break was only weeks away. The scent of spring flowers filled the air as I walked home from school, and I basked in the warmth of the afternoon sun. For a few minutes, I felt happy—like a normal girl with a normal life.

Who can I be today?

I pretended to be the sister of Ponyboy Curtis from *The Outsiders*. In my imagination I was his twin sister, Toni, and our brothers would come and protect me from anything that threatened me. I smiled as I walked like she would have—brave, strong, protected, and tough. But then I rounded the corner of my block. At seeing the police cars lined up in front of Dad's shop and our apartment above it, I stopped. Toni Curtis evaporated, and bile rose up in my throat.

They had finally found my dad out.

The cars reminded me that my life wasn't even close to normal. What normal girl was met with a show of force from law enforcement when she came home from school? *Normal.* What a word. Someone once told me, "Normal is only a setting on a washer," as if it were an elusive thing no one could ever catch. But when you're in a never-ending storm of madness, you see normal as a unicorn you want to capture with all your being. Living in the chaos of having a mentally ill father was all I'd ever known, despite seeing glimpses of normalcy on television shows or in other families. Bottom line: I knew who I was and who I could never be.

While I was the daughter of the supposedly "cool" dad to many of my friends, what they thought they saw was nothing like what was true. They thought they wanted what I had until, like a Venus flytrap, they would be devoured.

Now, as I stood on my street, my heavy legs threatened to drop me to my knees. Somehow, I kept walking toward the building, instinctively knowing this was going to be bad. Really bad.

Breathe. Just breathe.

The police weren't in my dad's shop below our apartment, so I dashed up the stairwell that was through a side door of the building to the second floor. The pounding of my feet on the hardwood stairs exploded in my ears, and before I could reach the top, other footsteps staccato amid the hum of conversation.

Men were standing outside the apartment door, and the light from the back entry window made them into strange, moving silhouettes. One of the men held up his hand and asked what I wanted.

Peeking my head into the apartment, I somehow managed, "I live here."

Another man told him he could let me in.

When I eased into the apartment, my dad was calmly sitting in handcuffs on the couch while men tore through every room. In my bedroom, strangers rifled through my drawers. I fought anger, watching them touch my intimate things. Their voices mingled in a buzz as they talked back and forth about photographing this and that.

Nausea spread through my stomach. What was going on? Deep down I knew, but I wanted to pretend I didn't. But I knew. My father was a rapist, and he had finally been discovered. My whole life was on display for every man in that apartment to see. I was no longer just

Jenni, the reject. Now I was Jenni the daughter of a sex offender. And all of them knew.

If we had been in a taller building, I would have hurled myself out the window and plummeted to my death. Scum seemed to sully the inside of my brain, making it hard to think. The men made it worse by touching my things and invading my life.

Dad's voice cut through my haze. "Can I talk to her?"

The men eyed each other warily as they debated it. Finally, they agreed that it wouldn't hurt anyone. Well, except me. They didn't realize it would undoubtedly hurt me.

Two men led us out to the hallway outside of the front door of the apartment.

"You know I'm innocent," my dad babbled. "You know I didn't do anything wrong."

I scowled. Was he seriously trying to tell me, of all people, how innocent he was? I didn't have words to reply. I just nodded like I believed him, even though my mind was screaming, *What am I going to do now? What am I going to do?* I was sixteen with nowhere else to go, and my only parent was about to be taken away. As painful as my life had been, my dad was my constant. I had no one else.

One of the men gave me the contents of my dad's pockets, including the silver pocketknife he always carried. It felt heavy in my hands as I stared at it and traced the smooth metal.

Dad continued to ramble insane denials that he'd done anything wrong. Finally, he ran out of words like a deflated balloon, and they took him back inside. They informed me I was not allowed in the "crime scene," so I walked back downstairs to the shop. Police were there too, going through everything. Sitting at the metal desk at the front of the shop, I watched as my life fell apart.

The men there made less noise as they rummaged through things. They were almost drowned out by the banging overhead in the apartment.

Someone stomped down the stairs. A young man—probably in his late twenties with a military-style cut to his blond hair—burst through the shop door and fixed his angry gaze on me. A shorter police officer, about the same age but with dark hair, followed him. "You!" The blond man pointed at me. "How could you do this?"

Shrinking back, I whispered, "What?"

"You lured those girls here for your father, didn't you? You're just as guilty as he is!" He was screaming so loud that a little burst of spit shot out.

I shook my head quickly, raising my arms for the blow I was sure was coming. "No, I didn't!" But deep down, I did feel guilty. Guilty for not having a clue about how I could have stopped him, guilty for being alive, guilty for being the daughter of a rapist, guilty for being born.

The dark-haired officer grabbed the man's arm.

"You're old enough to know better!" the man bellowed. "You helped him do this!"

"Stop it. Calm down!" The officer stepped in front of him to keep him away from me. "Leave her alone. She didn't do anything."

The blond man spun around and walked out the shop door. His steps pounded like nails into my head as he went back up the steps.

The air was so thick I struggled to breathe. The intervening officer simply gave me a pitiful look, shook his head, and slipped out the door.

The inflicted cut was deep, and I sat emotionally bleeding out. The accusations of things I couldn't control and didn't do washed over me in waves. Bizarrely, a part of me wanted to fall down at the blond officer's feet and admit he was right, even though logically I hadn't done anything wrong.

More noise on the stairs was followed by movement around the front door as uniformed officers and detectives appeared on the sidewalk. I rushed to the door just in time to see my dad being escorted to an awaiting cruiser.

"Keep the shop open!" he yelled to me. "I'll be back soon!"

All of them got into their cruisers and unmarked vehicles. None of them asked if I had anywhere to go. At sixteen, I wasn't old enough to be on my own. There was no call to a social worker, no reassurances that they would help me in any way, nothing. I stood on the step of the shop and watched as the cars pulled away. Not even my dad seemed to care that I was left there alone. He didn't even offer a glance through the back window.

By that evening, I knew that Dad wasn't going to be coming home anytime soon.

My fingers tapped on the phone as I wondered if I should call my granny or a cousin who would be able to take me in. After some thought, I forced myself to call my cousin Emma to see if I could stay the night with her. There was no way I would sleep in the apartment by myself.

Emma was a niece of my birth mother, Rosa. She lived in Collins, but my dad had never allowed me to see her. To him, all of Rosa's family members were dirt. The alternative to calling Emma was letting my granny know all the gory details of her son's arrest, and I couldn't bring myself to have that conversation.

So, I went back upstairs to the ransacked apartment and packed some clothes. Dropping down onto the very spot where my dad had just sat in handcuffs, I took in the mess. I wanted to fade into the flowery wallpaper and disappear. What they did to my belongings was a violation, but I knew that didn't matter to anyone but me. Tears slid down my face, despite how I'd vowed not to cry.

Stop crying, you weakling! I jumped up, grabbed what I'd need, locked the apartment door, and went down to the sidewalk to wait for Emma's husband to pick me up.

When we arrived at Emma's, she was standing on the balcony of her apartment breezeway, gazing down. Her flaxen-haired little boy sat on her hip. Smiling, she offered a wave and then gave me an awkward one-armed hug when I reached her.

Gone was the fifteen-year-old cousin I had once known, and in her place was a graceful, smiling mother of almost twenty. She waved me into the apartment, her face alight with barely contained joy. The toddler had the same clear blue eyes and a smile that lit up his entire face.

With the barrier of my dad removed, we talked about old times. Soon we were giggling and then laughing until we cried. The roar of our outrageous stories filled the room. It seemed obscene to be laughing at a time like this, but it released something in me I couldn't explain.

I could breathe easier with Emma. She was family I hadn't been allowed to have. We shared blood and an experience with Dad that others didn't understand. She had tried to save me from him once, and now here I sat at the place I tried to escape to four years before. I wished my dad would never get out, and with that thought, a new wave of guilt hit me. What kind of daughter was I?

Our laughter was cut short by sharp knocking on the door. I froze when the door opened and Rosa strolled in. Having heard about my dad's arrest, she'd wasted no time in driving down from Cincinnati, where she was living. Emma greeted her with a hug, so apparently they had more of a relationship than my mother and I had ever had.

Great. I eyed Rosa with suspicion. I hadn't seen her in four years, with my last memories of her being when I was in the sixth grade.

She didn't mention Dad or the elephant in the room—his crimes. Instead, she stared at me like she was waiting for something. My affection, maybe? Relief at her being there? Whatever it was, I wasn't about to give anything to her, not one bit. If she'd expected me to throw myself into her arms, I hoped she wasn't holding her breath.

part one

CHAPTER 1

beginning of the end

One year prior....

Collins, Kentucky, is a seemingly genteel town that sits at the foothills of the Appalachian Mountains. It's a small, sleepy town that moves at a slow pace except on Friday nights, when everyone comes out to watch the high school football team, the Stinger. Everyone knows everyone, and people often met up at the drive-up root beer stand to get chili dogs and fries, brought out by the car-hops. On Saturday nights, folks would drive around the local shopping center in a circle just trying to see who else was there.

During the summer before I started ninth grade, my dad found an apartment on Main Street, in an old boxy building that housed a shoe repair shop on one side and a large open space to the right that became my dad's electronics shop. Allied TV Service was born.

On the second floor were six small apartments. The one that became ours had one bedroom, a small bathroom, a living room, and a kitchen. The bedroom went to my dad, while I got a bed in the buttery-yellow kitchen.

The kitchen had a length of large windows that overlooked the intersection of the two main roads in Collins. I would lay awake at night and gaze out at that intersection and wish I was anywhere else but there.

My favorite view from that window was at night when it rained. I'd watch the traffic light change from green to yellow to red, and its glow would reflect off the pavement like a show. In the quiet of the kitchen, I'd find some solace.

Fortunately, the high school was within walking distance of the apartment, so I didn't need to ride a bus or figure out other ways to get to school. Throughout the week I was required to work in Dad's shop after school hours, answering the phone and greeting customers when they dropped stuff off or picked it up. The business was divided into two sections by a two-by-four wall frame covered by wood paneling on one side. A curtain hung in the doorway cut out between the two spaces.

Once, my dad got so drunk while working that when a customer came in to pick up something, he burst out from behind the curtain, dancing around the space without a care in the world. After several moments of swaying to the music, he disappeared back behind the curtain. The customer stared at me in disbelief. I simply swallowed, red-faced, and finished taking his money, ignoring my dad so the customer could leave and I could crawl under the desk in embarrassment.

No one knew my father was mentally ill. No one knew that he did drugs and drank himself into a stupor. Family didn't want to see my dad as ill either, only as willfully difficult. Since they put him in that category, they apparently didn't think I needed their help.

His diagnosis of schizophrenia came while he had been married to my birth mother before I was born. They were living in another state, and he attempted to have her committed to a mental health facility, convinced she was insane. The doctor at the hospital watched interactions between them and eventually released her and diagnosed my dad. That diagnosis went nowhere, however. I guess, for everyone around him, it seemed an unimportant detail in their scheme of surviving.

My dad and mom had a violent relationship that eventually had my her fleeing from life with him and me. I was fourteen months old and didn't know of her existence until many years later. Starting high school is awkward for any kid, but when a girl doesn't have a female influence in her life, it's even more challenging. Plus, I was artsy, considered weird, and not popular. So I kept my head down and kept to myself. Books became a way for me to escape the chaos of my home life.

At the end of my freshman year, my dad met a young man who would be the unwilling link to the implosion of my life. Brad was in his early twenties, a muscular former football player, and good-looking with curly dark hair and deep-brown foreboding eyes. He was well known and liked in our small town. Brad needed some work done on a television and came into our shop to get it fixed. They struck up an immediate friendship even though almost thirty years different in age. I blushed every time he came in, as he would meet my gaze with a wink.

Soon my dad learned of parties Brad would throw at his house on the weekends. Lots of teens and young adults wanted to experience all the crazy fun that seemed to happen there. Dad talked Brad into having one of those parties at our apartment, telling him that he would buy all that was needed to supply the gathering. I was told to go to the skating rink for the night. My dad didn't care how I got there or how I paid to get in, but I had to leave.

That one night had my dad hooked.

Parties took on epic proportions in our apartment, and he no longer cared if I was there or not. Dad was fifty, but he told everyone he was thirty-nine and tried to act as young as the ones coming over. He allowed everyone to drink if they wanted to, age didn't matter. Late one evening, someone cracked out a joint and started passing it around. My dad saw it and said nothing. So, drugs became okay at these parties.

Brad suddenly stopped coming around, but his friends kept coming over. Not only his friends but classmates of mine. Then they would bring "their" friends who were even younger than me. With my dad providing everything, more and more people came over. He became the lauded hero to the young, playing the part of the adult who seemingly understood their angst and desire to let loose. Dad was right there with them, drinking, smoking pot, and playing strip poker. He became a man interested in what they were doing, a listening ear and friend. Later I would recognize what he was doing. Like a predator seducing its prey, he was grooming them for the price for all this freedom.

Depression gripped me hard. As much as my dad showered attention on the young people who came to the parties, I was ignored—

unless I did something wrong. In that case, I was met with responses like, "Dummy," "Idiot," "You're just like your mother," and the ever clever, "You shouldn't have ever been born."

While I could manage the weekdays of the mental abuse my dad would heap on me, the weekends were entirely different. I would come home from the skating rink to find our house filled with some of my friends and some folks we didn't know. I had nowhere to retreat, since my bed was in the kitchen. I learned to drink my cares away so I wouldn't have to feel anything. Numbness was better, and blackouts became routine. To people I didn't know, I was the daughter of the cool dad. Except no one really cared about me—they just wanted in on the party—and barely noticed that I was there. So I began to disappear into the bottle.

Along with drinking, Dad began to use drugs with all of the party attendees. That didn't help his mental status at all. He began to use his fists to punch me if he didn't like what I said. It started as I stood washing dishes one evening, a chore I despised. As I let the water run over a clean plate, my dad came in.

Leaning into the refrigerator, he grabbed a beer. "I think Brad's girl-friend likes me," he announced as he shut the door, his chest puffing out.

I shook my head. "Isn't she too young for you?"

Suddenly my mouth exploded with pain from a blow I took to the face. My arm jerked up out of the water and threw it everywhere as I grasped my mouth and turned to face my dad, who stood with his fists clenched.

"Why did you hit me?" I asked.

His fist came at me again and landed on the side of my head, knocking me to the ground. Tears spilled from my eyes as I curled up on the floor.

He leaned over me, his breath hot on my face. "This is what I'm going to do anytime you say a word I don't like. Do you hear me?"

I held onto my head as the world spun, then nodded.

He relaxed a little and straightened. "Good. Now get these dishes done. We have company coming over."

He disappeared into the living room, leaving me a shaking mess on the kitchen floor. In the past, my dad had whipped me with leather belt, but had never struck me with his fist. This was new, but somehow, I forced the fear down along with everything else I'd ever felt. In a few hours, I could cry myself to sleep like I did almost every night, but for now, I needed to get up and finish the dishes before he hit me again.

With shaky hands I pulled myself up to the counter and finished the dishes. My head swam and my lip felt thick. I gently licked it and couldn't imagine what it actually looked like.

After that, I avoided him as much as I could. If I couldn't get away, I'd drink. The only thing I lived for were the times that took me out of the desperate moments.

Stupid drunk?
Check.
Shoving emotions down?
Check.
Slowly dying?
Check.

I lost faith that anything was going to change the course I was on. I was going to die in this place. Whether or not I did so by my own hand or not was yet to be seen. What I knew was I was barely holding on. My insides were a jumbled mess most of the time. I'm not even sure how I made it through classes. I cheated on school work whenever I had the chance; there just seemed to be no other way to make it because of the storm that swirled around me.

When I couldn't drink, books became my escape. I discovered that during the day, I could easily get away from my life by reading. I read anything by SE Hinton, Ben Bova, and any other author that spoke to me. *The Outsiders* became what I lived through. I became Toni Curtis, twin sister to Ponyboy Curtis.

I loved the escape so much that I started writing fan fiction, or sequels to those books, and sharing them around school. I even designed the covers. I talked a few friends into that same sort of make-believe, and we took pictures around the school, posing like tough girls complete with black T-shirts and jeans.

The parties continued, drawing people I knew and didn't know. One Saturday morning after a long night of partying, I gazed at my dad in disbelief, feeling suddenly emboldened to speak. "You know, Dad, you shouldn't be doing all this with my friends," I pointed out, like the age difference wasn't obvious to him.

His face blazed red. "Your friends?" he spat. "*Your* friends? Those are *my* friends, and I'll do what I want with them. Now shut up, you idiot!"

He was right. Those few people I knew as friends were now his friends. I was just collateral noise around the main event.

It wasn't uncommon to see strip poker with thirteen-year-old girls and sixteen-year-old boys. Inevitably, the girls would end up covered by a towel to try to keep their modesty, but it never worked. Sometimes couples would slip into the bedroom, including my dad with girls. I never knew exactly what was going on, but I had an idea.

One evening during one of the parties, my dad came into the kitchen, where I sat on my bed staring out the window at the traffic light. "Jenny, come help me," he demanded and pointed to the bedroom.

I slid off the bed and walked by the hordes of kids sitting around smoking pot. A cloud of smoke hung heavy in the room.

As I stepped through the bedroom doorway, a shirtless boy was fastening his pants. Beside him a girl lay passed out, vomit spilling out of her mouth onto the pillow. Her shirt was hiked up to her neck, and her bra was bunched at the top of her chest, exposing her breasts.

At seeing me, the boy raced past as he pulled his shirt over his head.

I slammed shut the part of my brain that told me what had happened to her. Denial was a refuge, and I wanted to stay there. It was the only place I could be safe. The alternative was...yeah, I wasn't going there.

"Help me lift her up," Dad said.

After we had taken off her soiled shirt, removed the pillowcase, and placed her back on the bed, my dad handed me the shirt. "Wash it out and hang it up to dry."

"Okay."

But he didn't move when I headed for the door.

"Close the door," he ordered, pointing to it.

My last image of my dad was of him standing beside the passed-out girl.

As I washed out the shirt in the bathroom, my brain was panicked and confused and a million other emotions I couldn't process. A welcomed blankness arrived, and I was able to finish and hang up the shirt. It was a shirt she should have been wearing. Instead, it was dripping puddles of water in a tub and she was without it in the other room.

When I walked back into the kitchen, I grabbed a beer from the fridge and drank it as quickly as I could, pausing only long enough to let the air out of my stomach. Then I downed another, only stopping when the desire to cut my wrists passed.

I didn't want to live anymore.

Not like this.

Not with him.

I wanted the terror and depression to stop. I *wanted* my dad to stop. But this was my life, and it was never going to change.

My hazy brain cried out to God, begging him to save me. Because if he didn't, I was going to die, one way or another. Either by my own hand or by the hand of life.

At the skating rink I went to every Friday and Saturday night, I made friends with sisters, Shay and Lizzie, who were thirteen and fifteen. They had long chestnut-colored hair and striking blue eyes and seemed very feminine, something I wanted to learn about since I felt more like a boy than a girl. Their uncle always came to the rink with them and meandered around the video games and benches or sat stoically in the concession area at the back table. He was tall and menacing, wearing sunglasses even when it was dark, and you never knew where he was looking. There was no warmth from him, and his demeanor made him seem more like a guard than a family member. Warning bells sounded in my head whenever I was around him.

I was only acquainted with the girls, but they showed up to the apartment a few times for my dad's parties, morphing from people I knew into members of his crew of friends. When they invited me to stay overnight at their house, I was surprised that my dad agreed. So, one night after skating, we all crammed into a small car and headed for their house.

The tiny rooms of their home were crammed with people. *Who are all these people?* I wondered. Their uncle took a seat in the corner of a room, while Shay and Lizzie's mother perpetually moved around the house as if unsettled, a cigarette constantly hanging from her mouth. The ash landed everywhere, but she didn't seem to care.

The house's front room housed a round pot-belly stove that radiated heat. A couple of lanky men I didn't know were there as well, sitting and talking, one with barely any teeth. None of them ever spoke to the uncle.

Glancing around the room, I noticed how odd the wallpaper was, with its mismatched patterns of black against brown. It was only when I looked closer that I saw that the black was actually roaches. They were trailing up the walls, sometimes moving around ones that had been squished but left there like they were a warning to the others.

My skin began to crawl at the thought of sleeping here, and fear wrapped around me like a vice. The uncle with his shaded eyes, the family that seemingly didn't care that I was there, and the bugs by the hundreds were too much. I wanted to go home. But I had no one to call to come get me.

When night came, darkness seemed to settle even on the inside of the house. The lamps barely touched the veil of tension in there. I couldn't put my finger on it, but I was relieved when we eventually went to bed. I knew the quicker I went to sleep, the quicker morning would come.

With the lights turned out, I lay staring up at the ceiling, wondering if a bug would land on me or perhaps crawl into bed with me. Thankfully, Shay and Lizzie nestled me between them in their double bed. So maybe the bugs would get to them first.

After a while, I could tell they were asleep, but I stayed awake for the remainder of the night, waiting until night gave way to the coming sunrise.

When I finally got home, I stripped off all of my clothing and took the hottest shower my skin could bear. I crammed my clothes into the laundry basket, so glad to be away from that house.

One afternoon not long after that, my dad suggested, "Hey, why don't you invite Shay and Lizzie here to stay the night?"

I glanced around, then leveled my gaze at him. "Where would they sleep?"

"Oh, I could let you and them sleep in the bedroom. What do you think?" He was relaxed but careful in his words, something my dad never seemed to be.

I blinked a few times. "Well...sure, I'll ask."

It wouldn't seem so weird for them to come here. After all, our tiny apartment was much cleaner than their house. A week later on a Saturday afternoon, their uncle followed them into my dad's shop.

"Jenny, why don't you take the girls upstairs while we talk," he suggested, indicating the big man with shaded eyes.

"Okay," I agreed and led them to the upstairs. Shay was babbling about her skates and if we might get to go later.

I shrugged.

Minutes later, we were still in the living room talking about skating when my dad waltzed in. "Jenny, I need you to go check the mail."

I scowled. Our mail was delivered to the post office, about two miles away. I typically put on my skates to take the trip so it would go faster, but it was a trek none the less. "But Dad, Shay and Lizzie—"

"They'll be fine," he insisted. "Go on."

I looked at them and reluctantly went to pull my skates from under my bed in the kitchen. As I began to lace them, my dad joked with them. Joked. Actually joked.

"Dad, we wanted to go skating tonight, and if you take us, we can check the mail on the way there," I told him.

A storm appeared on his face. "Shut up, stupid! Do as you're told!"

I nodded and quickly made my way to the door. When I glanced back at the three of them, Shay and Lizzie looked relaxed, like this was no big deal.

"On second thought, why don't you walk," Dad said before I got out the door.

Walk? "Why? I mean, I'm faster when I skate."

"Walk," my dad seethed.

I dropped into a chair and unlaced the skates, then put my sneakers back on. As I shut the door behind me, Shay giggled.

With every step, I felt like someone was stabbing me. How my dad had treated me in front of them was completely embarrassing. The hot summer air seemed to amplify my misery, and I angrily wiped the sweat from my forehead.

On foot, the trip would take me at least an hour. Wearing skates, I could have done it in about thirty minutes. Why did he want me to walk? It didn't make any sense.

When I got back from the post office, I could hear the shower running. Shay was in the bedroom gazing into the mirror while applying makeup. She stopped and gave me a smile. Lizzie sat lazily on the couch watching TV, her clothing slightly askew. That meant my dad was in the shower. That was odd. He never took a shower in the middle of the day.

I laid the mail beside the TV and turned to look at both of them. It didn't seem to matter that I was back. Shay's brief smile was the only acknowledgment I got.

The shower turned off, and my dad emerged from the bathroom with wet hair and a towel around him. He walked into the bedroom and booted Shay out with a smile and a slap to her back end.

I wanted to die.

Shay watched as the door closed and then turned to me. "We're going skating tonight. Your dad is going to take us."

"He is?" My dad never took me to the skating rink. It was always up to me to find my way and to beg enough money from friends to get in. So this was unexpected. But it was also one less thing to worry about.

"Yep," she confirmed with an exaggerated nod as she slapped her brush on her hand.

Well, okay then.

The ride to the skating rink was weird. Shay and I sat in the back of the van while Lizzie had the passenger seat. Dad made odd jokes, ones he mostly laughed about while we all just listened. I was embarrassed, but Lizzie and Shay seemed indifferent, like they were elsewhere in their heads. I guess that was good. I didn't want them to know just how strange my dad really was.

As we got out of the van, my dad handed me a five-dollar bill.

I stared at him. Really? He was giving me money? I almost didn't know what to do for a split second, but I took it and rushed out before he could change his mind. Five dollars would get me in to the rink till 10 and let me buy a soft drink and maybe some popcorn. If I stayed till midnight, the full five would be gone on admission alone. Still, him handing me any type of money made me feel rich.

When we walked into the skating rink, Shay and Lizzie's uncle stood inside the doors as if he'd been waiting for them. They met him and chatted, but I went to sit on a bench nearby. Shay nodded a few times but didn't seem to say much. Eventually the uncle turned and walked away.

I shuddered and went to put on my skates.

At the night's end, Shay and Lizzie waved to their uncle as if to say goodbye and we headed out to wait for my dad. Suddenly the uncle appeared and remained standing near us as we waited. I wanted him to go away. Far, far away.

We waited in the tense silence until my dad's van pulled up. I made a beeline for the passenger side, with Shay and Lizzie right on my heels.

"I'll be there to get them in the morning," the uncle growled to my dad.

"Sure," Dad agreed and gave him a dismissive wave.

The uncle grasped the door before Lizzie could shut it. "They will be ready by nine."

My dad suddenly seemed more alert. "They will."

This seemed to appease the uncle, who let the door close, and we pulled away. I stole a glance behind me to see that mountain of a man watching us leave.

When we arrived home, I discovered the sleeping arrangements were different. My dad volunteered to take the couch and give his bed to Shay and Lizzie. I would sleep in my bed in the kitchen as always.

In the morning we said goodbye, and I wondered if this was how sleepovers were supposed to go. A cold sort of dance around each other? No intimate talk, no sharing of feelings? It was more like the girls were simply co-existing in a space I occupied.

On a different Saturday night when I got home from skating, my dad wasn't in the apartment. I grabbed a pillow off of my bed, puffed it up, and laid down on the floor. Right as I was about to fall asleep, my dad burst inside. Shay slipped in behind him.

A few moments later, I glanced behind me and Shay was taking off her bra. I turned around, lay back down, and squeezed my eyes closed.

This was not happening. It just wasn't. Mercifully, my senses completely shut down and I blacked out. I don't recall how I made it to bed, I don't recall when Shay left, and I don't even recall what happened the next morning. I was—and still am—glad for that black hole.

CHAPTER 2

slow burn

While the weekends and evenings were hard, Saturday mornings were a tiny bright spot in my week. Mainly because I knew it was time to do laundry. Laundry? Collins's small laundromat sat on the next block from the apartment, on the other side of the Food Fair grocery store. It would take a couple of trips for me to get all the laundry there, but eventually I could settle in and proceed.

My dad always gave me a roll of quarters to wash and dry the clothes. If I put enough clothes in a load, I usually had enough to play a video game or maybe by a soft drink or a candy bar from the vending machine. But I had to be smart about how I did it.

Joycee Pike worked at the laundromat and oddly her incredibly tall husband and quiet son typically came and hung out with her as she worked. Joycee was no more than 5'2" with medium-length curly red hair, she was kind and wore a smile most of the time. Part of her job was to wash other people's clothes, and she taught me how to fold clothes in a way that made sense. I would study how she did things and mimic her movements. She became somewhat of a surrogate mother to me, at least for a few hours a week and I drank it in having a woman around me.

Her sixteen-year-old son Joshua was incredibly shy. He would eye me with curiosity as he retreated to playing the arcade game that sat in the corner. His wavy hair was always in dire need of a cut and curled up over his ears, and his eyes were the clearest blue I had ever seen, which contrasted against his perpetually flushed cheeks.

One day I ventured over. "Hi, can I play with you?" I asked, holding one of my prized extra quarters.

He studied me for a moment, seemingly considering whether or not I was a serial killer. "Sure," he said and stepped back.

"I'm Jenni. With an 'I'," I replied. It wasn't like the change of the spelling of "Jenny" meant anything to anyone, but I had recently did that to let people know it was short for Jennifer.

"I'm Joshua." He stuck out his hand, and we shook and started a friendship. At that moment, the laundromat became another refuge for me, like the skating rink.

Even on days other than Saturday, I would amble over to see if Joycee was working—and, by default, Joshua. He would either be playing video games or sitting in the front seat of his parent's station wagon, but eventually he'd come and talk to me while I stood with his mom. I always had to be quick so my dad wouldn't realize I was gone. Not that he cared what I did, but this was my own little part of the world, and I didn't want him invading it. Whenever I went out somewhere and couldn't adequately explain where I'd been, he accused me of being a whore, so I treaded carefully.

Joshua and I became fast friends. Laughing at stupid stuff as we sat on the parking barrier in front of the laundromat, my thoughts of suicide would retreat in the presence of the sun that was Joshua Pike. Later, he would tell me that he'd heard rumors about my dad, and while he'd wanted to help, he was in the same boat as me, clueless as to how save me from the terrifying person that was my father. So, he just was a friend to me through it. I don't blame him for not knowing how to help me, it was beyond any type of experience that anyone ever talked about.

I believe Joshua and his family were sent by God to help me through those difficult days. I lived for the moment of the Pike family arriving at work. I would even stumble over on some Saturday mornings, half-drunk from the night before, to see Joshua.

A rhythm began to take shape in my life. Skating, school, hanging at the laundromat, rinse, repeat. As time passed, I began to drink more heavily, depending on the alcohol to take effect enough that I didn't care what was happening around me.

The itch to kill myself became almost unbearable when I wasn't with the Pikes. Death seemed like the only way out. Who else was going to save me? No one ever gave me a second glance or asked if I was okay. Not a relative, not a friend, not even the myriad of teachers or adults in my life. Because of my larger than life, hair trigger angry, mentally ill dad, I believe people found it easier to tell themselves I was "probably" okay.

At one point, my dad decided it was time to have *the talk* with me— although his interpretation of that was much different from what other kids heard, I'm sure. When I got home from school one afternoon, my dad made me sit on the couch.

"Now, I want you to watch this," he said. "This is what a girl is supposed to do for a man." He pushed a tape into the VCR and hit play.

When the porn started on the screen, I shrank back. My heartbeat was so loud in my ears I could barely think, and my face felt like it was fire. I wanted to look away from what I was seeing. Who was I kidding anyway? My father had been into porn for a lot of years, hadn't cared to have sex with a girl with me in the room, and didn't care if people came to his parties and saw the deplorable things he had done. Yet, it was another horrifying thing to be instructed about what I was to do to a man via the sickening and alluring images on the television. I was taken back to being seven years old when my first exposure to pornography began. I was filled with so much shame.

I finally turned away, and he yelled, "Watch! You're to do that if you want to please a man. Understand?"

I nodded but wanted to puke. He made me sit there and watch movie after movie until I understood my role as a female with a male. I was to sexually please them in every way I could.

Finally, my dad seemed satisfied that he had done his duty and let me get up. The door to the bathroom had just closed when I lost the contents of my stomach in the toilet. I couldn't get the images out of my head. And my dad wanted me to do that?

As I came out of the bathroom with my head swimming, my dad sat on the couch like he was waiting on me. After getting up, he tried to have sex with me under the "guise" of a massage. Thank God, I was able to get away and out the door.

I stumbled to the laundromat, hoping Joshua would be there. I was so relieved that he was. If he knew something was wrong, he never asked. He simply handed me a quarter and stood with me as I tried to play a video game—which of course I couldn't. But I did try with shaking hands.

Winter arrived, and I was in dire need of a coat. My dad didn't like to spend money on me, though. As far as he was concerned, his money was for him and his needs. I only ate and slept at the apartment by default. So I bundled up with layers of clothing and a light jacket to make the walk to school.

One evening, a friend of an older boy I knew saw my predicament as I stood in front of the skating rink trying to bum a ride home. The winter air was ripping through my clothes, and I shivered uncontrollably.

"So, Jenni, where's your coat?" Derek asked.

"I don't have one," I shot back with more irritation than I intended. Heat then flooded my face. I had a crush on Derek, and for him to notice was embarrassing.

"Want to wear mine?" he offered.

Was he kidding? Derek had a Honda motorcycle racing jacket. It was paneled in white, black, and blue, with *Honda* emblazoned down the sleeves and on the back. Lined with a dark-blue fake fur, I thought it was the coolest thing I'd ever seen.

Before I could answer, he unzipped the jacket and offered it to me with a smile. I could feel the warmth of it on my hand from where it had been against his shoulders. At first, I held it out, not sure what to do.

Derek nodded as he stood there in short sleeves. "Go on now. Put it on," he said.

I took off my paper-thin jacket and slid my arms into it. It smelled of him and was so warm. I held back the tears as I zipped it up. It completely blocked out the wind. Then realization hit me as he stood there. "But now you'll be cold." I began to unzip it.

His hand shot out to stop me. "No, you keep it for now. I'll get it back from you later. And I'm okay. I have another coat at home."

Before I could answer, one of Derek's close friends came out the skating-rink door with his little sister in tow. He looked at me and then at Derek but didn't comment on it. "Ready to go?" he asked Derek.

"Yep, just waiting on you," he said, then winked at me. "We're giving Jenni a ride home too." Derek inclined his head toward the car, and the four of us got in.

The entire drive home, I kept hugging myself, worrying over when I'd have to give it back. But sitting there in the jacket, I felt like the queen of the world.

At the end of the winter, I tried to give back the jacket.

Derek held out his hands to me. "Nah, you keep it," he said and smiled.

Tears pricked my eyes at his generosity. The coat became the ever-present reminder that kindness did still exist in the world.

A girl's sweet sixteen is supposed to be a birthday full of promise. Sometimes it involves a new car from her parents, a party, and accolades for the hope of a bright future ahead for the celebrant. Not for me. My sixteenth birthday "celebration" ended with a suicide attempt.

Months of parties, sex, drugs, and abuse coalesced into a depression so dark that I could hardly extract myself. I wanted someone to see me and realize I needed help. The words would swell in my gut and be expressed in cuts that I inflicted on myself to release the repressed cries. Cutting was the physical bleeding of an emotional hemorrhage. But even cutting was not enough.

Every morning I'd wake up, gaze at my reflection in the mirror, and think, *Today would be a good day to die.* Every moment in that apartment built into a profound desire to die. It hounded me every day. It would be the first thing I thought of when I woke up and the last thing I considered before falling asleep.

Suicide.

It was hard to face each day, hungry for salvation and seeing none. I began to exist in a way I could hardly express. My identity began to be a smeared, undefined image with no defined features. The current carried me away like a riptide. But instead of trying to swim, I embraced the desire to die. It became the one thing that would carry me to the elusive peace I so desperately wanted.

It would be my salvation.

It would be my way out.

And I accepted the thoughts of dying like it was my own personal savior.

My sixteenth birthday didn't fall on a weekend, but that didn't deter a skating-rink friend named John who was determined to make it a special day. He was like a surrogate brother of sorts who I trusted. "Come on, Jenni. We're going to celebrate your birthday," he announced as soon as I arrived at the rink.

I blinked. *We're going to celebrate my birthday?* "Okay," I agreed. But at my house we didn't celebrate anything anymore—not birthdays, not Christmas, nothing. My birthday would be a regular day to everyone except to my granny, who never forgot an important day.

Nevertheless, John urged me out to the parking lot. A couple of cars sat parked near the back of the lot, just beyond the reach of most of the lights. One of the vehicles was a VW bug that was owned by John's friend Brian. I always loved his car. It was souped up and had its exhaust stack sticking straight up out of the back so the car could go through the mud. The paint job was an inconsistent mess of color, but I didn't care.

Brian waited and smiled. He was seventeen and heavy-set, with shoulder-length dark hair, blue eyes, and a wide gap between his two front teeth. He laughed all the time, and even when things were grim would figure out a way to make things fun. I wondered if he was high most of the time.

Brian opened his car door, and sitting on the passenger seat were two cases of Little Kings and a bottle of vodka and orange juice. "Ta-da! Happy birthday!" he said.

"Yeah, happy birthday." John pulled me into a sloppy sideways hug.

"Thanks!" I couldn't wait for the numbness the alcohol was going to bring.

We started drinking, huddling down behind the cars whenever someone pulled up. I didn't care how anything tasted. The effect was what I was after.

Slowly the buzz hit. The knots inside me started to unwind. It was a nice illusion of peace, and I liked it. I drank even faster so I could just numb out. Then things started getting off kilter. What I didn't expect was for the profound sadness and loss to start seeping out of my cracks. I began to get sobby.

Another friend of mine, this one nicknamed Badger, pulled up and got out and hugged me. He pulled back and saw that I was completely undone, and didn't need to ask why. He knew everything that was going on with my dad and how unhappy I was. "Can I take her with me?" he asked Brian. "I'll try to calm her down."

Brian, who was completely high from smoking pot in between beers, didn't care one way or another. He was more fascinated with his hands and how funny they were shaped. John agreed. He knew Badger as well as I did and knew I'd be safe.

I weaved over to Badger's car and got into the passenger side. It smelled of cherries from the air freshener hanging around the rearview mirror.

He slipped into the driver's seat and looked over at me. "So, Jenni, where to?" His voice echoed around and took a few minutes to hit my brain.

For whatever reason, I needed to know about one person—Wayne Michaels. He was a boy I was deeply in love with, but the relationship was profoundly unrequited. Wayne and Badger hung out together. Both had a love of the military and getting high. "Have you seen Wayne lately?"

Badger snuck a look at me as he drove. "Now, honey, why the hell do you want to know about him?" He kept his eyes focused forward, watching the road.

"I love him," I said matter-of-factly.

"I know you do, but it's your birthday. You should be happy, not worried about him."

You should be happy.

Ha! No, I should be dead.

I thought about how much I loved Wayne and how alone I felt. I thought about how Wayne seemed to accentuate my aloneness in the world and emulate how everyone else seemed to me. I was a no one. Life was never going to change. I'd never be happy, and there wasn't a hope for anything else.

Suddenly, the courage to do the one thing I dreamt of doing came to me. I'd thought about dying so many times, about how to take my life and how I just wanted this overwhelming pain to go away. I wanted peace and didn't have it.

I looked over at the door and reached for the handle. We were cruising down the interstate, so if I jumped out, the landing would probably kill me. I just needed to jump out to my death. I could do that. Turning to Badger, I said, "This is where I get off." I jerked the car door opened and planted my feet to jump out.

My peace was just a landing away.

But something jerked me back into the car. Badger. He had me pinned down on the bench seat of his car with his muscular forearm. "What the fuck do you think you're doing?" he roared as he pulled over.

Fury rushed out of me as I struggled against him. "Let me out! Let me out!" I screamed as I kicked the windshield and out the open passenger door. He was ruining everything! I fought with everything my inebriated self had. In the end, I just wasn't strong enough.

The car came to a halt, and Badger threw the car into park hard. Jerked me up to sitting. "What was that about? Huh? Are you trying to kill yourself?"

"Yes!" And the tears came out so easily because the wall that typically held them in was gone. I was an exposed nerve to a hammer.

Badger's expression softened. "Come here," he whispered and pulled me to him. "It's going to be okay, Jenni. It's going to be okay." His arm rested around me as he caressed my arm.

Was it?

I cried uncontrollably into Badger's shirt as we sat on the side of the road.But I don't know if it was because I was devastated I didn't die or because I was relieved I had lived.

CHAPTER 3

unraveling

Even though my reputation for having the "cool dad" bought me credence with some people, to most I was still just a low-class nobody who dressed in boys' clothes most of the time. So I was shocked when I came home from the skating rink one evening to see there was no party happening but a cheerleader from my school and her friend were sitting on our couch drinking beer with my dad.

I slowly closed the door and eyed them.

"Hey, Jenni," Lana said cheerfully, raising her beer and causing it to spill a bit.

"Hi," I replied softly and walked toward my bed in the kitchen.

She giggled along with the other girl.

My dad's gregarious laugh joined in. "Jenni, get me another beer!"

Pulling a cold can from the refrigerator, I tried to figure out what Lana and her friend were doing here. I had no idea who the other girl was. She was a rather tall, full-figured girl who towered over Lana.

My dad jerked the beer out of my hand when I held it out to him. "Go away."

The only thing I could think to do was go into the bedroom. Pulling the record player from underneath the bed, I put on a Loverboy album and turned it up to drown out the conversation out front.

If I cut my wrists, how long would it take to bleed out? I wondered. *Would they find me in time? What happens when you die? Would I be found looking ghostly white? Would I go to heaven right away or purgatory?* I shook my head. *Wherever I go will be better than this.*

Most of the kids who came to my house weren't from the popular crowd, so I had no worries that anything would get to the popular people and make me even more low-class. Yet here sat a cheerleader, giggling with my dad and drinking.

Does bleeding to death really hurt or not? TV makes it like you just fall asleep, but would my heart try to beat with no blood and be painful?

I let myself get lost in the music. As I turned the album over to play it again, the door to the apartment opened and I could hear the voice of a new friend of my dad's. A few moments later, I heard loud scuffling and then Lana and her friend burst into the room. They slammed the door and fumbled with the knob to lock it.

I jumped up from the bed. "What?"

Before she could answer, my dad called through the door, "Oh, come on now. Don't be shy. Let's have some fun."

"Yeah, girls!" his friend added. "Come on out here and let's get to know each other a bit."

Lana's wild eyes met mine. "Help us," she pled, backing away from the door.

But what could I do? I was one girl. I shrank back from her pleas, as I had no power. I hated who I was and who my dad was.

My dad was pounding so hard on the door that that the top of it moved back and forth. I thought for sure the lock was going to break.

Lana's friend was breathing heavy, and I worried she was having a panic attack.

Dad continued to try to cajole them to come out. They barricaded the door with their bodies, eventually slumping down to sitting. After a while, the banging subsided, but muffled laughing echoed as they continued to yell to the girls.

I slid down the wall, mortified. My dad expected sex from them in exchange for the beer. Going by Lana's terrified expression, I knew she hadn't been aware of that. Apparently, she didn't know *all* the rumors about my dad.

Under the weight of the situation, I began to break. Try as I did, I couldn't hold myself together. Tears streamed down my face and I began to shake. "I want to die," I told them. "Like cut my wrists or take a bunch of pills or something. I'm tired of living like this."

"Does this happen a lot?" Lana asked, shocked.

"Yes." I wiped away the tears that kept coming. "I really want to kill myself." In a small way, it was a relief to admit that out loud. To anyone.

Lana's voice softened. "Jenni, don't say that."

I buried my face in my hands and cried. Here I was trapped in a room with two girls I barely knew, while my dad and his friend waited to have sex with them. I had nowhere to go, no place of safety, and I wanted to die. "He hits me." My muffled voice echoed against my skin. I didn't look up to see their reaction.

"That's awful," the other girl replied.

I nodded and listened to them consider their options on how to get away.

"There's only one way out," I said. "I'll try to sneak you guys out somehow."

"Our parents think we're spending the night at the other's house," the girl offered. "If we disappear, no one will know."

"You aren't going to disappear." But in truth, I didn't know what was going to happen.

After about an hour and a half of listening to them weigh their options, I realized it was silent in the living room. I got up and unlocked the door as quietly as I could. After a glance at their worried faces, I turned the handle and cracked the door. My dad was asleep on the floor, and his friend lay on his side on the couch, snoring.

I motioned for the girls to follow me, and we tiptoed to the door of the apartment. As soon as I opened it, they rushed out and didn't look back. I couldn't blame them. I wanted to run away as well, but I was stuck here. Forever. Unless I could work up the nerve to actually kill myself.

After grabbing a beer, I went back into the bedroom, sat on the edge of the bed, and downed the beer as quickly as I could.

My head hit the pillow and I cried myself to sleep.

"Jenni, you're wanted in the principal's office," my teacher said, glancing at me, after reading the note handed to her by an errand boy.

All eyes turned to me as I stood. I couldn't imagine why the principal wanted me.

The hallways of my high school were mostly silent, except for the occasional muted words of teachers in their respective classrooms. I could hear my feet shuffling along the industrial carpet.

When I stepped into the principal's office, I let the secretary know I had been called down. She didn't even get up from her desk as she inclined her head toward a woman who stood to my right, talking to Mr. Tipton. They spoke in hushed tones, and he had his arms folded and his head bowed as he nodded along with what she was saying.

Recognition flashed across his face when he saw me. "You guys can talk in our conference room." He spoke like I should know what he was talking about, then motioned me forward and pointed down a small hallway to a room with a table and chairs.

The woman was short with wiry reddish hair and glasses. A grin spread across her face when our gazes met. "Hello, Jenni," she said once we were in the room.

"Hi."

She indicated a chair.

I dropped into it and sat back, waiting for her to explain what was going on.

She took the chair across from me and pulled out a pad of paper and pen. "I'm Sandra Branson. I'm a social worker. Do you prefer Jennifer or Jenni?"

I took her offered hand and shook it. My mouth was so dry I almost didn't know how to move my lips and speak. "Jenni is fine."

She gave a gentle smile. "Jenni it is." From her impressive bag on the floor, she produced a folder and laid it on the table. As she opened it, she asked, "Are you having a good day?"

I shrugged. "I guess."

"Good." She placed her clasped hands on the open folder and

studied me. "Jenni, I received a phone call about you and your well-being and just wanted to talk to you."

People were concerned about me? Squirming in my seat, I tried to beat down the butterflies batting around in my gut like they were made of steel.

"Well, we got a report that your dad was having parties at your house."

My vision tilted and for a moment I couldn't breathe. My body reflexively remembered to do it, but I struggled to take in a normal breath. "Who told you that?"

She smiled again. "It doesn't matter who it was. The important thing is whether it's true or not. Can we talk about that?"

Can. We. Talk. About. It?

Really? To a stranger?

All the warning bells sounded in my head, and I wanted to bolt from the room and never look back. Somehow, I remained tethered to the chair. I stared at her for a long time, never speaking a word. Sweat beaded on my upper lip and I brushed it away.

"Jenni, it's fine if it's true. I just want to make sure you're safe. Are you okay?"

Her patience amazed me. She just sat there waiting as I tried to form words that I could say out loud instead of the constant stream of admissions going on in my head.

My dad has sex with my friends.

My dad hits me.

My dad hurts me.

My dad calls me stupid. Maybe I am stupid.

My dad hurts everyone.

I want to die. Please let me die.

"Jenni?" She reached her hand toward me. "Has your dad ever hit you?"

A piece of my wall crumbled inside, bruising my defenses. She knew. My God, somehow she knew. I didn't think to lie in that moment. I was desperate for someone to know what I was going through. To just admit the truth and speak the horrible things into the light. I looked down at my hands. "Yes," I whispered.

"I thought so." She moved some papers around. "We also have reports that your father is allowing your friends to drink and smoke pot in his apartment. Is that true?"

Just how much did she know? Was she going to ask me about the sex with kids my age too? I wasn't exactly sure what kind of crime it was my dad was committing, but I knew he shouldn't be messing with kids. Was she going to ask about that next? I felt like I was already going to hell for admitting that my dad hit me, so I wasn't sure if I should admit this too.

"It doesn't matter if you tell me yes or no, Jenni. We already have several reports that he does. I just wanted to hear from you if it was the case."

She was so much like a mother sitting across from me, disarming me with kindness. I actually liked her and wanted to tell her everything. Deciding to only go as far as she asked, I traced the lines of my palm with my thumb to hide how badly my hands were shaking. "Yes."

This seemed to please her. "I see. I was told that kids your age go to these parties. Is that right?"

"Yes."

I was going to hell. Literally going to hell. But I couldn't reconcile the relief at admitting it with the condemnation at telling.

Her pen clicked and she began to write. I couldn't make out the words and didn't want to. I wanted to crawl under the table and hide.

Then she asked a question that was like a lifeline: "Is there anywhere you can live if I can get you out of your father's house?"

I looked at her, blinking spastically, and said the only place I could think of. "I can live with my granny."

"Good, good." She wrote down something else. After a few brief sentences, she pulled out a card and slid it across the table toward me. "Call me if anything gets...bad in your house. Okay? Night or day."

I picked it up and tried to beat down the small amount of hope she seemed to be offering me. Reading all the numbers listed on it, I thought about how organized and tidy her writing was and how the benign colors lined up on the business card. Here was what could save me if I needed it to. I could live with my granny? How could this woman manage it? Surely my dad wouldn't allow it.

As I walked out of the room with her, the principal pointed me back to my class with a note, as if things were routine.

The card burned a hole in my pocket as I walked home that afternoon. Throughout the night, I couldn't sleep. I kept thinking one singular feeling over and over again. I was guilty. Because I had betrayed my dad. I was a horrible daughter. If he got into trouble, I was to blame. And what would my dad do to me once he found out? I needed to fix what I had done.

The next day, I found my way to the phone in the school library and called Sandra. As soon as she answered, I blurted, "I lied."

"Jenni Butler?"

"Yes, it's me. And I wanted you to know that everything I told you yesterday was a lie. If anyone asks me about it, I'll say it wasn't true." I hoped she couldn't see through me to the truth. I had to protect him, and this was the only way I could think to do it.

"Okay, Jenni, okay," she said. "I'll just forget everything you told me."

Relief washed over me. "Good," I breathed hard against the receiver. I had dodged a bullet. I hung up feeling like my world was going to return to its skewed version of normal. But at least I hadn't betrayed the only person I had.

Even though he was guilty and I knew it, I couldn't shift the guilt from me to him. It was as if my brain continually blamed me in such a way that it wasn't even logical to me that he was guilty and he had done this all on his own. All I could see was me and how I had cause all this.

Even now, looking back at this, I see that I wasn't protecting my father and his crimes as much as I was grasping onto the one thing I knew was certain—the one person I had in my life—and that was my father. As much as I wanted him to stop, I didn't see an alternative, not even in the social worker coming to see me.

The unwritten rule of the Appalachian Mountains was that you protected your own no matter what. Blood was blood, and if you betrayed it for whatever reason, you were the most heinous criminal and deserving of death.

Looking back, I know it was fear of betrayal and terror that drove me to recant. At the time I wasn't sure what all drove me, but I at least felt as if I couldn't sell-out my father even though I was desperate for someone to find out and help me out of the situation. But I couldn't bring myself to be a willing participant in my own saving if it meant turning in my father.

🦪

Linda Staunton scrutinized me over the squeaky conveyor belt of the grocery market checkout. Her makeup was so thick that I wondered how her face could move—cakey foundation, thick lip gloss, and frosted-blue eye shadow. What she lacked in height she made up for in attitude and big, perfectly teased highlighted hair, which must have given her another three inches in height.

As I handed over my money to pay for my candy, she casually said, "You know, I hear they're investigating your father for the parties he has up there." She inclined her head in the direction of our apartment.

The change she'd handed me tumbled between my fingers to the conveyor belt as I gaped at her. I whirled around to the long wall behind me, as if I could see right through it to our building. She muttered under her breath and stopped the belt before it ate the coins at the edge.

A high-pitched squeal sounded in my ears while my blood ran cold. I gaped like a fish sucking in air. "What? What do you mean?"

She glared as she picked up the coins to hand them to me. "Don't play stupid, Jenni. Everyone knows what your father is doing over there. Except now the police know too." With a tilt of her head, she offered a haughty grin, as if she needed to gauge my reaction, and dropped the coins into my hand.

Soft thudding told me someone stood behind me in line tossing their groceries onto the sticky black belt. I couldn't turn my head to look at them because I stood transfixed, staring at her like a bird at a snake.

The conveyor belt squeaked as it started up.

"Have a nice day," she said with a dismissive little chuckle and began to ring up the items from the customer behind me.

The only thought I had was that I had to tell my dad. He had to be aware of what was coming. Maybe he'd stop and we could try to live a normal life. Could the threat of trouble do that? Could he even conjure normal anyway? Normal never happened, so why would I even consider that it would start now?

The door chimed as I rushed into the shop. Dad was sitting at his desk, gazing through a magnifying glass on a spider arm, soldering something. Wisps of smoke drifted up each time he touched the item on the counter. MTV echoed through the shop.

I stumbled up to the window portion of the partition, my hands shaking and feeling the candy bar wrapper sticking to my sweaty skin. "Dad?" The spicy scent of burning solder filled my nose.

He didn't look up. "Hmm?" Another trail of twisting cloud wafted up and dissipated.

"Linda Staunton just told me that you're being investigated by the police for the parties you're having."

He lifted his gaze to mine. After a few seconds, an eyebrow raised. "What did she say?"

"Just that you were being investigated—by the police," I further clarified, as if a person could be investigated by anyone else.

He sat back in his chair. "I haven't done anything wrong."

Yeah, right.

My brain exploded with accusations. Screamed, actually. But they were stopped cold by the implications of him getting in trouble. If he were arrested, where would I go? What would happen to me?

Then my brain seized up with the realization that maybe I'd caused all of this. That by me telling anyone anything, I had caused him to be investigated. I fought the urge to throw up as I thought about the social worker.

My dad tapped his finger on his desk, deep in thought. Something bad was coming. No doubt about it. The light at the end of the tunnel was a train, and I was about to be flattened.

God, please help me. Please.

He got up and exited the shop to go upstairs. A minute later, he returned with a large box and dropped it on the desk with a thud. Photo envelopes brimmed over the edge, maybe twenty in all. He rushed to the back of the shop and was gone a few moments before returning with short black bottles with gray lids. He crammed the canisters of negatives into the box. "Jenni, you need to do something for me. You need to go out back and burn all of this."

"What is it?" I asked.

"Shut up stupid. Just go burn it already." Dad handed me a lighter. "Do it quickly."

I picked up the box, made my way to the paved area behind the building, and opened it. I almost threw up.

Inside the box, below the envelopes, were stacks of photos of young girls and some flat negatives. The top photo was of a blonde girl I knew...posing...nude. A weird sort of grin was on her face. Leaning down I picked it up and held the corner out to light it on fire. Before long, I had a small hill of ashes as I burned image after image of nude photos of girls, some as young as twelve.

Swallowing to keep down bile, I fought the urge to run, but I held steadfastly to the task of burning all those photos and the negatives until I hit the bottom of the box. Nothing was left to destroy.

Watching the blaze, a chorus of thoughts rushed so quick through my brain that I couldn't coherently gather them. All the things I knew were going on with the girls jumped up at me in vivid color. I couldn't deny what I was seeing. It was another reminder that I was living in a literal hell.

The flames scorched my feeble attempts to deny reality, in spite of what I saw with my own eyes and heard with my own ears. My dad had sex with young girls. Watching photos of the victims melt away in this pile, my mind was overwhelmed. I couldn't process it. I couldn't face the fact of what my dad was doing, and I just wanted to fly away. The only escape I could ever see was dying. I couldn't reconcile my feeling of hatred for my dad and wanting to protect the only parent I had. Why couldn't someone take me away from the horrid things happening around me?

The only thing I allowed myself to do was breathe. Just breathe in and breathe out. I couldn't even consider his guilt or allow myself to feel the crash of waves that ripped at my insides. My dad was a monster— having sex with girls younger than me. The pictures didn't need to confirm it for me, but to deny what I heard him doing on the couch behind me or what I had seen him doing at parties with high and drunk girls was no longer an option. I wanted to shut down my brain.

Just breathe. Just breathe and only breathe.

A little over a week later, my dad was arrested.

CHAPTER 4

daughter of a rapist

The headline on the front page of the local paper leaped out at me from the counter of the carryout: *Merchant held in rape, sodomy cases.*

My fingers traced the headline with dread. Stepping to the side, I picked up the small paper and unfolded it to see the entire article. Each word brought bile up into my mouth.

There was nothing like having your world exposed, even though the heinous details in the article seemed innocuously detached. My name didn't appear anywhere, but only one family in our small town had my last name, so everyone would know. *Everyone.*

I couldn't defend this. I couldn't go to each person who read the article and try to explain any of it. What could I explain anyway? That although the details were vague, there were more sinister facts that had not been told. It would be like pointing out a broken toenail on a bodiless leg. The bigger concern should be where the body was. Everyone was looking at the broken toenail, but I knew all about the body. My life in this small town would never be the same.

The first blatantly not true line was the one giving my dad's age—thirty-nine. Since I was sixteen, that would have made him thirteen when I was born. Not true at all. As if his age would make his actions more conscionable.

A second line in the article caught my eye: "Also, contrary to a rumor circulating about the case, Lewis said there were no known pictures taken of the victims. 'I didn't find any pictures,' he said." My heart sank because I knew the truth. The one thing I was absolutely guilty of was destroying evidence.

🦪

A few days after my dad's arrest, my cousin Emma, who I was now living with, talked me into going back to school. As I closed the door to her small car behind me, I stopped and stared at the door. The bell had already rung, so a few kids rushed in to not be counted as late even though they were, but none seemed to notice me. That was a small victory.

My fingers clenched my backpack while I willed my feet to move. My brain was a whirl of emotions, wondering if anyone had read the newspaper article. I was on the edge of walking back into one of the few elements of my life that seemed routine, but fear had me questioning how my dad's arrest would affect my life at school.

"Call me if you need anything, okay?" Emma called through the open passenger-side window.

If I needed anything? I needed to run away. I needed to not feel anything. I needed to be held and told it was okay. But it wasn't okay. It was never going to be okay. Did I need anything? More than anyone could ever give me at this point. So what could I say?

I needed to die. Then this would all be over forever. My dad wouldn't be able to hurt me, the pain would be gone, and I wouldn't feel anything. I wished I'd never been born. "Yeah, okay," I muttered and forced myself forward. With one foot in front of the other, I succeeded in getting into the building.

My legs felt like lead as I moved through the almost-empty hallway. Relief washed over me at being late, because I didn't have to face anyone. After opening my locker, I retrieved my books and headed to first period. I couldn't focus. A thick fog flooded my head, and things around me seemed warped and cartoonish. It was worse than being drunk.

When I opened the door to my classroom, it was early enough that small conversations were still going on. Without looking at anyone, I slipped into my chair, hoping I wasn't noticed.

I let my eyes creep up to look around. My heart sank as I noticed a boy looking at me, horrified. He turned to the girl behind him and whispered something. Her head snapped up, and she glared at me. I knew what she was thinking. What was I doing there? Shouldn't I be in jail or something? I mean, if my dad was guilty, wasn't I? I pushed away the detective's accusing words.

My relief came when the teacher brought the class to order. I took in a deep breath and opened my notebook, then pulled out a pen and started to draw random doodles. But I couldn't understand the teacher. I knew he was talking, saying something that should be of importance to me, but I couldn't translate his words. It was a hum—musical spoken words that were in a foreign language.

What *was* I doing here? Why had I decided to come to school? I'd thought that acting as if things were normal would make them normal. *Normal.* Such a word. When had things ever been normal for me? I had a dad who claimed he talked to angels, who told me about the pending alien invasion—and who, just for kicks, raped girls on our living room couch.

I would never be normal. I would always be the daughter of a monster. Under the weight of the stares, I felt like I must've had the word *freak* stamped on my forehead.

Finally, the bell rang, and I rushed out of the room, almost knocking down the guy in front of me to make it out the door. I was running, I knew. But I couldn't slow down. My legs moved of their own accord, pushing me toward an open hallway that was now no safer than my life with my dad. My life was exposed for all to see—all the gory, horrible details, like a macabre side show.

At my locker, I sucked in air, trying to catch my breath. Why couldn't I breathe right? The warped world seemed to have invisible hands wrapping themselves around my neck, cutting off the oxygen.

I turned just in time to see a group of kids huddled together, whispering and pointing at me. So much for safety in the routine of school.

Who was I kidding? The stain on me was obvious for anyone to see. No amount of pretending was going to change that.

After cramming my books into my locker, I slammed the door. I took in a deep breath, determining that I wasn't going to run and I wasn't going to rush. I was going to walk like a sane person. The floor felt magnetic, and just moving my feet took immense effort.

The whispers and pointing followed me, although different faces channeled it as I walked. Everyone knew. *Everyone.* They had all decided my fate, my identity, in the blink of an eye. I was a criminal. No one said the word directly to me, but their shushed accusations were a crescendo of final judgment over me.

Breathe, just breathe and keep walking.

I chest was tight. I fought down the urge to throw up.

Just keep walking and don't look at anyone else.

Eventually I made it to the principal's office and stood at the long counter that separated the students from the staff, watching the flurry of activity of students coming and going and the incessant ringing of a phone. I wanted to open my mouth to say something, but no words came out.

Once the office was empty of students, Ms. Tipton realized I stood waiting, picking at my cuticles. "Can I help you?" she asked without actually looking at me.

My brain eventually managed to compose a clear sentence. "Can I call my cousin?" I croaked. "I'm not feeling well."

She studied me. What was on her face? Grief? Shock? Maybe sympathy? "Of course," she said and moved to open the gateway between the staff area and public area. She directed me to a phone sitting on an unmanned desk.

I dialed Emma's number and asked her to come get me. She must have agreed, because I hung up the phone with a small sense of relief.

A week later, I took my finals in the principal's office. Ms. Tipton met me at the front counter and pointed me back to the same room I had talked to the social worker in. Surprisingly, she shut the door. Apparently, she didn't care if I cheated, not that I would anyway. But still. Maybe it was her way of being apologetic or permissive due to my situation. Whatever the reason, it reinforced my isolation from everyone.

I sat down at the table and looked at the pages before me. All my classes were represented there—English, Biology, Social Studies, Algebra, and Home Economics. Alongside them were the corresponding multiple-choice answer sheets and the trusty #2 pencils.

I picked up the first exam and began to read. A sick feeling ran through me like hot oil. It was as if I had never taken any of the classes before—like I was a Spanish-speaking student taking my tests in English. Was I stroking out? I tried to pick out the most relevant parts to understand what the tests required, but I couldn't figure out what it was asking.

I laid my head down, letting the coolness of the table soothe me. I was going to get through this, wasn't I? I could pass these and make it to my junior year. But honestly, I wasn't so sure. Just like everything else, this seemingly simple task took on monumental proportions. A small voice told me it was all just further reassurance of how stupid and worthless I was.

Lifting my head, I rubbed the moisture away from my eyes and determined to do something besides try to figure out the answers, which seemed hopeless. The carbon of the pencil smoothly colored in the circles in a lovely design of my choosing.

When I was done with the five sheets, they made a fantastic piece of art. I knew I would fail the year, but at that point I was beyond caring. I was beyond everything, spun together in a loose bundle resembling a girl. Next school year could have been twenty years away for all it mattered to me. It was too far away to mean anything real. If I failed, so what? Besides, my life was already a mess. What was one more thing?

I stood up, gathered my sheets, and returned to the front desk. Ms. Tipton was reviewing papers with a boy who seemed uninspired but listened out of obligation. I waited for the student to walk out before handing her my tests.

She smiled at me. "Are you all finished, dear?"

I grinned and nodded, pretending to be okay.

"All right, dear. We'll see you next year," she said. "Have a good summer."

I watched her for a minute, wondering if I'd be back here next year —or even alive. It was an optimistic thought that I might actually make it through this, and one I didn't necessarily believe. "Thank you, Ms. Tipton," I whispered, then tacked on, "for everything."

Her kind eyes met mine. "You're welcome." Her tone almost added a "sweetheart" on the end, but she let the unspoken word hang there. Pity pinched her face. I desperately needed it but fiercely didn't want it.

I turned and all but ran out the door. The hallways were quiet since the other students were in their classes. God, I was so jealous of their normalcy.

I looked over at the open cafeteria beside the library. So many lunches I'd spent in there, so many conversations and laughter. Now I was leaving, and the uncertainty of my return loomed. Inwardly, I whispered goodbye to a school that had been my home for the first two years of high school. Somehow, I knew I'd never be back.

Shockingly, I passed my tenth grade, albeit with D's. I believe the teachers had mercy on me and, rather than add another struggle to my life by failing me, let me pass by the skin of my teeth. But I knew the truth: I had failed. Unless, of course, my beautiful design on the answer sheets had actually marked the right answers.

The heavy door to the county jail opened with a massive creek, and Emma and I slipped from the heat of the day into the chilly air of the concrete building. To our left was a desk with a glass partition and a small tray that moved back and forth to allow people to sign in and send the clipboard back to the awaiting worker.

Emma motioned me forward. "I'm not going in. I'll stay out here with Henry," she said and headed for the plastic chairs lined up in a waiting area.

My stomach clenched. Forcing a breath in, I walked toward the officer waiting impatiently for me to sign in. My fingers could barely form the letters of my dad's name on the paper. I pressed my lips together as I finished. My gaze lifted to the officer waiting for approval.

The deputy nodded, then came out and led me to a heavy iron door. His keys clanked against the iron as he disengaged the lock.

As I was led into a small room, I noticed one side was almost all glass. The prisoners in the large communal bay could see me there waiting for my dad to be brought to the adjoining other side of a high-countered barrier finished off by glass. Only a small round hole provided the ability to hold a conversation. There were no chairs, so these visits had no intention of offering any comfort. Chair or no chair, my legs itched to run, but I forced them to stay still.

The yelling inside the holding bay echoed through the glass, with men asking if I wanted to have sex or could lift my shirt for them. I felt the blood drain from my face with each word of profanity. I focused on my feet.

Moments later, my dad was brought to the other side of the divider. He looked remarkably the same, wearing the same clothing he was arrested in.

He came right to the hole. "Are you keeping the shop open?"

I shook my head. "Emma can't take me down after school. Her husband uses her car in the evening."

His face reddened and he swore. "I'm going to lose business, and this is all your fault! If your friends hadn't accused me, I wouldn't be here. You know I'm innocent."

I glared at him. No response I could have given would've made any sense.

His movements became frenetic, and he began to almost chant, "This is all your fault." Over and over again he said it. Mixed in was, "They were your friends."

Never mind that when he had started having people over, I told him it wasn't a good idea. My mouth recalled the numbness after his punch in reply to my warning. Back then it was, "They're my friends, not yours." But now that he was in jail, the blame was being put on me.

It was another shot across the bow of the guilt boat I sailed in. A perverse cruise to hell with a dash of blame.

While my dad spat at me, the chorus from the prisoners continued.

My vision became hazy, and I couldn't hear him. His mouth moved, but I could only hear my own breathing. Hot wax seemed to be flowing over me, insulating me. I managed to nod a few times when I thought I should.

Slowly my hearing returned—just in time to catch that my dad was being assigned a public defender, who'd start working on getting him bail. That started a whole new sick battle in my head. I didn't want him out, I wanted him away from me. But I was stuck so deep in a web that there was no way to get free.

His parting words were that I needed to find a way to get down to the shop and open it. But what could I do? I could sit in that cold shop in silence and hope no one ever came in, that was it. It wasn't like I could do the repairs. I had no transportation anyway. Torn between what he demanded and what I couldn't do, I just turned away.

When I joined Emma in the waiting room, she stood up holding Henry and offered a weak smile but didn't ask me anything. I watched the landscape go by on the ride home, considering that if he were released, I should go ahead and take my own life. Who would care if I died anyway? Would I try pills this time? Cut my wrist? What would be the most effective?

What if he remained in jail? Maybe I could be free of him—maybe. I didn't hold out much hope. My dad's gift was finding ways out of his messes. Nothing could hold him. He'd probably be right back out, ruling my life like he owned me.

I just hoped that if he got out, I'd have the courage to do what I needed to do.

***

"Are you sure?" I asked my dad's public defender after he had produced the list of girls who had accused my dad. I looked at the list, letting my fingertips roll over the penned writing.

Most of the girls I knew and hung around with. They had been to my house and went skating with me. These were people I called friends. But I couldn't weigh out all of the truth or falseness of what was there. The only one on that list who I didn't know was the girl who had thrown up on herself after passing out on the bed. I shook my head, trying to not remember.

The final two were Shay and Lizzie, the girls sold by their uncle. Voices became muffled around me as in my head I heard the noises of the fifteen-year-old and my dad on the couch behind me having sex. Nausea threatened, and I glanced at the garbage can by the public defender's desk.

Knowing that most of the girls on the list were people I knew made it hard to separate myself from my dad. Their accusing him of anything seemed like accusing me, and my friends wouldn't do that, would they?

My brain began to melt the things I remembered into an evaporating fog—a sort of brainwashed mentality. The words my dad had repeatedly pressured me with every phone call, every visit, every letter was a mantra: "You know I'm not guilty." A small voice within me said he was right. Somehow, I'd strangely started believing it.

An iron wall came down, pressing the secret knowledge behind it. The emotion remained. The feelings that continuously told me I deserved to be dead. That no one loved me and I would be better off dead.

The public defender's name was Larry Spears, and he was young, no older than in his late twenties. He had cropped curly brown hair and blue eyes behind long lashes. I thought he was cute, and that made him a little easier to talk to. Plus, he was supposed to be on my dad's side, which meant he was on my side—another point for him.

Larry looked across his desk at me. I kept staring at the names, trying so hard to make sense of their involvement. "Your father has asserted he is innocent, and that was the plea we entered into in court. He says you can testify that their accusations are all fabrications."

"Dad says they're lying," I stated matter-of-factly.

Larry nodded. "But what we need to know is why. What reason could they have for lying?"

I was asking myself the same thing. Why lie? Then I considered the act of rape. When I thought of rape, I thought of a violent act, of someone forcing themselves on someone else. Had I ever seen that? No, I'm not sure I had. But I had seen coercion.

Wait...Had I? No, I hadn't, because my dad was innocent...right? Right. Innocent. Nothing happened. Absolutely nothing happened.

If he was innocent, then nothing happened. Nothing at all.

A flash of a memory of one girl in particular clawed at my brain, but I wouldn't let it in. The sounds pounded inside my head. Then there was the burning pictures...

No!

I shuddered, and Larry stopped talking. Had he been talking? I shook my head. I wasn't going to tell him that while my brain began washing itself in blankness, my gut twisted in knots.

Without realizing it, a defensive part of my brain began to mentally floss my memories, pulling those scenes out and feverishly tossing them to the side. The events morphed into shadows in my head. It happened so seamlessly that I didn't even realize what was happening. My mind was forcing me to survive without my conscious consent.

Make it go away. Please, God in heaven, if you are there, please save me and make it go away. Even better, God, please let me die.

"Jenni?" Larry said.

I jolted from my thoughts. "What?" I sat up straighter.

"I asked, do you know why they would be lying?" His eyes bore into mine.

"No idea," I whispered.

"Well," he said as he began gathering his papers, "we'll meet again. Think about it, and if you come up with anything, let me know."

He shook my hand with a smile, which surprised me. He seemed like he might actually like me. Most people seemed to regard me with distain. But not Larry, he was on our side.

Maybe I am likable?

No, Jenni, you are not. You are not a good person, so who would like you?

No, Jenni, you are the daughter of a rapist.

CHAPTER 5

coping

I woke up in the middle of the night. Where was I? My heart pounded so hard I thought it would explode out of my chest. At realizing I didn't recognize anything around me, I sat up.

Flashes rushed through my mind. Feeling my dad's hands on me. Sounds of him having sex behind me on the couch. The arrest. My trying to jump out of a moving car to kill myself. Screaming. Someone had been screaming.

Only a nightmare. I was at Emma's and nowhere near my dad. I let out a long breath and lay back down on my cot. The nightmare had been so vivid that I couldn't dismiss it as an overactive imagination. No, it seemed as real as the beating of my heart. But my dad was innocent —right?

I must be losing my mind.

The moonlight flooded in the window and spilled onto the vision of Henry sleeping in his bed across the room. His small arms lay in weird directions, and his mopped blonde hair was a mess. He slept peacefully, blissfully unaware of anything amiss. He was so beautiful and innocent. I wanted to be him.

My breath caught, and I sat up again and angled my body against the wall, pulling my knees up. I felt like an animal trapped in a cage with no physical barriers. I had lost a father who, while scary, had been my one consistently present parent. Never mind that Rosa had remained in Collins, staying with friends but encountering me at different times and demanding I live with her. But she was an absolute stranger who had never been a part of my life. Realistically, I had no parents, no home, and no safety. The prick of tears started before I could stop it.

I grabbed my pillow and buried my face into its softness and let go, sobbing until my crying became hiccups and my breaths were shudders. Couldn't I just pretend I was someone else for a while—be someone other than who I was?

It felt like a knife was tearing through my chest. Why was all this happening? Why? I so desperately wished to have normal parents. Ones who would care about me and what I thought. Who would actually buy me clothes when I needed them, who would hold me when I was afraid, and who would somehow convince me they would fight all the demons in my life and love me just because I was theirs. I wished I was wanted. I desperately wanted to be loved, cherished. But I wasn't. My mother had never wanted me, and I was a burden to my psychotic dad. Why had God allowed me to be born?

God, if you are real, please just kill me. Please. Let me close my eyes and never wake up. Please. Please, God.

I sat awake and succumbed to a weird desire to tug on my eyelashes. One by one, I jerked each lash out. The small prick released the frustration inside. I sat there tugging on my lashes until I felt calm enough to go back to sleep. Finally, exhaustion overtook me and I drifted off to sleep.

The next morning, I stumbled into the small kitchen.

Emma was fixing breakfast for Henry as he played with his toys at the table. "Hey, good morning," she said as I sat down. Then turning to me, she stared. "What happened to your eyes? All your eyelashes are...gone."

I shrugged. "I had a reaction to some mascara."

"It caused all your eyelashes to fall out?"

I nodded, hoping she wouldn't figure out what I'd done.

"Well, don't use that again." She continued to work on breakfast. "I hope they grow back soon. Your eyes look weird." She stirred the egg into a heap. "So," she went on, drawing out the word, "there's a hearing for your custody. It's some sort of emergency hearing for Rosa to get you."

The air seemed thin, and I couldn't get a breath in. "Emma, she can't get me. She can't."

"I know," she said without looking at me. "But she's the only parent left. They won't give you to me."

"Why not? I'm sixteen. Don't I have a say? I mean, I don't even know her." My heart fluttered so hard I thought it was going to stop. It was one thing to have that quick visit with her the night dad got arrested, but where had she been when I really needed her? "I won't go. I'd rather die first. Or I'll run away. They can't keep me." I stood up so quick that I shook the table and knocked over the chair.

Henry froze, grasping a small car as he gazed up at me.

Emma jerked around, still holding the spatula. "Stop. No, you won't run away. We're going to figure this out. Trust me." Her blue eyes sparked with determination.

I heaved in air. Eventually I nodded and let out a sigh as I righted the chair. As I sat down again, I wondered if Rosa could actually pull this off and keep me with her. It was like gazing up at a guillotine blade hovering above my head, ready to split me in two. No amount of wanting seemed to help.

"You know," Emma said slowly while continuing to cook, "we could just call the judge and see if he'd be willing to let you stay here."

My words almost caught in my throat. "Could we even do that?"

She shrugged. "Maybe. Why not?"

A ray of light broke through the dense clouds around me. Dare I hope? Would a judge actually listen to anything we had to say? After all, I was the daughter of a rapist, was poor, and had no influence. Who would care what I thought? No one had thus far. Desperately I held onto Emma's faith. If I couldn't hope. I'd just hold on to hers.

After breakfast, Emma was an unstoppable force. Just like that, she found the judge's number, which she dialed. Her eyes roamed around the room as she tapped the phone. Suddenly she sat up straight and cleared her throat. After answering some basic questions, she said, "Okay," and handed me the phone. "He wants to talk to you."

My hands shook so much that I almost dropped the phone. "Hello?"

His voice was deep, commanding, and devoid of any hint of what he was thinking about the situation. All the questions were blunt and probing. He asked about my mother, our relationship, and how I was related to Emma.

When he seemed satisfied, he wanted to speak to Emma again. After handing her the phone, I jumped up to walk off all the bugs that seemed to be crawling up and down my arms and legs.

They seemed to talk forever, but eventually she hung up with a grim look on her face. "I don't know," she said in answer to my lifted hands. "We wait."

Emma had scrambled to get whatever government assistance she could after obtaining temporary custody of me. One of those benefits was a program called the Job Training Partnership Act, or the JTPA. I qualified to get a summer job at an outpatient medical facility that provided assistance to the mentally challenged. I'd never had a real job before, and I so looked forward to earning my own money.

On the scheduled day, I reported to the director of the facility, dressed in the only pair of good jeans I had and a decent-looking top. I wanted to make a good impression, and kept smoothing out invisible wrinkles in hopes that I would look good enough.

I was ushered into her office for my "interview." I'd been approved to work there but still had to go through the actual interview process. After we shook hands, she motioned for me to sit down.

I looked around at the certifications on her walls, all ornately framed and displayed as treasures. Her large desk was covered with stacks of papers, books, and letters. Lowering herself into her chair, she smiled at me.

This was good. A smile was good. I sat up as straight as I could and tried to pretend I had confidence to do this job, whatever it was going to be. I honestly didn't care what I'd be doing, I was so eager to work and earn money.

"So, I have your application here, and I see you've never had a job before."

"No, I haven't. This will be my first job." I grinned, trying to appear friendly.

She nodded and continued to read. "We're going to have you work in our daycare area. We have special needs children who we teach from eight a.m. to twelve p.m. every day. You'll be a teacher's helper."

My stomach leaped. A teacher's helper? Oh, that sounded so exciting! I wanted to tell her I could start today. It took all I had not to bounce up and down, but I managed to contain my excitement.

"You'll start on Monday. You can wear jeans but no shorts. Make sure your clothes are clean, with no holes or stains. Okay?"

"Okay." I grinned again.

She weakly smiled back, almost a little bored. Then she looked down and continued reading. A deep frown crossed her face. "Butler...Butler," she muttered to herself as if she were searching her mind. Then she looked up. "Is your father John Butler?"

I weakly nodded.

She said nothing more about it, but I knew. She was mentally making the connection from him to me. It seemed I'd never be free of him.

As summer began, Emma's family and I settled into a new place. The public housing authority allowed us to move to a townhouse with three bedrooms, and it was genuinely nice and almost like a regular house. I had my own bedroom, so I could close my door and not have to worry about changing in the bathroom. It felt so extravagant.

Even though Emma was only twenty, she tried to make my life fit into hers as much as possible. It was challenging to be sure. She had been married for five years and had a four-year-old, and trying to take care of him and me wasn't something a twenty-year-old should have to do. Her husband, Richard, had a harder time adjusting to my being there. He struggled with supporting not only Emma and their son but also me. This was one more situation that I had no idea how to live in, but I honestly tried.

Months passed, and I worked my summer at the special needs daycare and earned enough money to buy all my school clothes for the coming year. It felt so good to have nice, new things. My dad had never felt the need to buy anything for me. To him, it was a waste of time and money, even though he had always been impeccably dressed. My coming by clothes had always been a chore, but this year was different. I felt like the queen of the world, wearing clothes I bought with money I earned.

At the end of the summer, I started my junior year at a large county school in the next town over. Some people there knew who I was, but I didn't have the same notoriety as at my previous school. I could breathe a little easier.

I had a few months of trying to figure out who my real friends were and if my dad had really done nothing, as he said. Emotionally, I was still struggling. I was cutting, suffering with trichotillomania, drinking, and living with the suicidal ideations that had never stopped. And I was profoundly depressed. No one seemed to take notice of that, because just like me, everyone around me operated in survival mode. We just kept going, never let our guard down, and certainly didn't wallow in our difficulties. My feelings about everything seemed more than what others could handle, so I simply kept it all to myself.

I know I could have benefited from counseling then, but I didn't know how to ask for help. And society around me was content to let me remain as I was. Everyone was failing me, intentionally or not.

Pretend, my brain whispered. *Just act like everything is all right. No one cares anyway.*

Walking down the halls of my new school, I tried to blend in. But that didn't last long. One day while I was washing my hands in the bathroom, four girls blocked the exit. Reilly, the only one I knew of, stood glaring at me, red-faced.

What she lacked in height, she made up for with her hot temper. I knew her brother from the skating rink but hadn't officially met her.

Her short haircut reminded me more of a boy's, and her stance was ridged and confrontational. She approached and pushed me hard. "I hear you want to fight me," she seethed between clenched teeth.

I shook my head. "No. No, I don't." Which was true. I barely knew her, let alone wanted to fight her.

She shoved me hard again, angling me back toward the wall. "Yeah, well, that isn't what I hear."

One of the other girls snickered.

Someone rushed out of a stall and burst out into the hallway, yelling, "Fight!"

All the blood seemed to rush from my face. Fear had my feet anchored in place at the thought that I was about to be beaten. Everything in me wanted to be brave, fierce even, but instead my own lack greeted me. I didn't want to fight. "Reilly, I don't know where you heard that, but I really don't want to fight you."

She sneered. "Ah, you're a chicken." Her fingers pressed hard into my shoulder.

Her posse behind her agreed, hooting about what a coward I was.

A short, blonde girl exited a stall, wide-eyed. The gurgling of water behind me confirmed that she was washing her hands. My mind quickly devised a plan. As the blonde girl approached the ones blocking the exit, they shifted to one side so she could pass. I bounded out into the hallway right behind her.

"Stop her!" Reilly screamed.

Shouts followed as the group of girls pursued me. I kept pushing my feet forward with a singular goal. The principal's office was now within sight. As I reached the door, all shouts behind me died.

Giving Reilly a quick look, I opened the door and went into the office. She glared at me and then disappeared as I closed the door behind me.

A girl with dark hair and thick glasses stood behind the counter sorting papers, and when she looked up at me, the girls on the other side of the glass retreated.

Clearing my throat, I asked, "Can I use your phone?"

She nodded and pointed to the end of the glossy counter.

For the second time in my very short period with Emma, I was calling her to save me from my classmates. She assured me she would come get me, and I settled into a chair to await her arrival.

When Emma walked into the office with Henry, she gave me a questioning look. She then asked to speak to the principal. She was quite a sight, holding her little boy's hand while making demands like a warrior.

Once the principal arrived, she made quick work of motioning me up and ordering me to tell him what had happened with Reilly. He guaranteed that he would address the matter quickly and sent the girl behind the counter to retrieve Reilly from her class.

You're such a snitch, I heard in my head. The accusation hit its mark. I had snitched out my dad, and now I had snitched out Reilly. Who else could I betray? I deserved to die. There was absolutely no redeeming value to my life. My birth was an accident of fate, and I really needed to rectify that. If only I had died on my sixteenth birthday.

When Emma was satisfied, she motioned for me to come with her and we exited the school. Reilly served a three-day suspension and never bothered me again.

Even though the experience with Reilly was done, life in a new school with a fresh start wasn't really all that fresh. I still endured the questions about my dad and the accusations that he was guilty.

Was he guilty?

I couldn't or wouldn't remember, and my head would hurt whenever I tried to think about specifics, so I didn't even try. For the sake of my sanity, I kept telling myself exactly what Dad said to me every time we spoke: "You know I didn't do this, Jenni. They are all lying. I'm innocent."

CHAPTER 6

the trial

The day finally came. The day I would have to watch everyone talk about what my dad was accused of—in public.

My stomach burned. Somehow, I managed to get dressed and leave with Emma to go to the courthouse. But my heart didn't stop beating and the world kept turning. My lungs still worked along with the thrumming of my heart. *God, please help me die*, I begged. *Please. Let my heart stop beating.*

Larry Spears waited for us at the front of the courthouse, dressed for the business at hand. His tie was precisely knotted, his wavy hair was gelled into place, and he carried his briefcase. All of our conversations, conjecture, and defense strategies were now going to be out in open court for all to see and hear.

I do not feel anything. I will not feel anything. Pretend, Jenni. Pretend.

Larry smiled as he greeted me. He was such a nice guy who seemed to enjoy what he did. What person enjoyed defending criminals? I didn't know anything about what an attorney did, but I couldn't imagine how he lived with himself. How did he turn it all off and not walk away from the experience sullied?

The building loomed like a tower about to collapse on me. My feet refused to obey for a moment. I forced a deep breath and began to move.

Larry held the door open, still with that same smile I couldn't understand. Noise assailed me as he pointed to marbled steps that wound up to the second floor. After a cursory exam by the security guards, we made our way up. "The defense witness room is just down the hall from the prosecution hall. But remember, you are not to talk to each other. Understood?" He led me to a door with a frosted window.

"Yes," I said. "But can't we sit in the courtroom during the trial?"

Larry shook his head. "Not if you're a witness. You can't hear what others say. But don't worry, it's going to be okay." He patted my arm and turned to go as I stepped into the room with Emma.

Nothing was going to be all right today. My life was either going to go back to hell or change irrevocably. My hands shook, so I balled up my fists in my lap after we sat down. My thoughts couldn't settle on which outcome it wanted more. I should want my dad acquitted of these false crimes. But the thoughts of sleeping on the bed in the kitchen, living with a man who beat me and had come onto me sexually was more than I could stomach.

Did he do anything else? Why can't I remember?

"I'm innocent, Jenni. Those girls are lying," replayed in my head. He did abuse me, but I probably deserved it.

Listen to him, Jenni. He wouldn't lie to you. He is your dad after all.

As I stared at my hands, a fierce desire rose up. I wanted the impossible thing. I wanted a home, parents, and safety. But that wasn't going to happen. I hated myself for always wanting that. I just needed to do things to distract me from that desire.

"Excuse me. Can I have a cigarette?" I asked a witness who was twirling a lighter on the table.

Emma frowned but said nothing as the boy handed a cigarette to me. My fingers rolled it over and over.

A burst of laughter came from the prosecution's witness room a door down. Hot fire licked up me. What was the laughing about? None of this was funny. *None.* I was losing my home and my dad, and it was all their fault.

It took all I had in me to sit down. I'm not sure how I got through the wait, but we were told by a deputy we were allowed to get a soft drink and go out front to smoke if we wanted to. I went back and forth between the front of the courthouse to smoke and back to our little room to wait.

On one trip back, I realized the sisters' "uncle" pimp stood outside of the prosecution witness room. He was wearing overalls, a black fedora, and dark sunglasses. I couldn't tell where he actually directed his eyes. Was he looking at me? Was he going to lash out and hit me or attack me in the hallway? The menace rolled off him in waves. I raced past him to the room.

What was he watching for? And why wasn't he in the room? I took one last fleeting look back as I ducked into the witness room.

Eventually, the deputy called my name. My breathing stopped and my hearing dulled. I swallowed hard and made my way to the courtroom.

The heavy door swung open, and all eyes turned to me. I followed the deputy past my dad on the left and the prosecutor on the right. Beyond the prosecutor sat the jury. They regarded me intently.

Pulling up straight, I squared my shoulders and walked forward. My throat threatened to close. *Do I look strong? I have to look strong.*

The witness chair was to the judge's left. An officer pointed to the chair, held out a Bible, and asked me to lay my hand on it. I swore to tell the truth, so help me God. One glance at the jury, and all I could think was, *Those people hate me and they want to destroy me. I probably deserve it.*

I sat down, and Larry stood up and adjusted his tie and jacket. For the first time, I glanced at dad. He stoically regarded me, but didn't smile or offer any type of encouragement. His lips pressed tight together. "I'm innocent, Jenni. Those girls are lying," I heard in my head.

I need to protect him. That's what good daughters do, and I want to be good.

His whittling away at me over the months had finally brainwashed me for this very moment. His words coalesced into a make-believe truth. For months, he'd began all of our conversations with, "You know I didn't do this, Jenni. You know I'm innocent."

In my head I would respond, "No. I know you're guilty," but I never had the nerve to say it out loud. I'd simply let his denial hang in the air. But he didn't say it just once. He said it during phone calls, during visits, and in letters—the constant "I'm innocent and they're lying" statement.

After months of his denials, it had become "They are your friends, and they are lying." This would send me off wanting to cut my own wrists. It hit a sore spot I always carried—I was guilty and my dad was innocent. I caused all of this. Somehow everything was my fault because I told a lie to the social worker. It was my fault I was alive. It was my fault because I was an evil piece of trash. I should find a gun and blow my brains out.

Their being my friends was my fault and they must be lying. I had to align myself with my dad to survive. I did, sitting in that chair staring at a jury, staring at strangers in uniform, and recalling the detective who had pointed in my face to enlighten me about my guilt at having friends at all. I wasn't safe, and so I should have known better.

Yes, I caused all of this, so I need to make it right. Instead of inwardly disagreeing with him, I began to agree. *Yes, you're innocent. Yes, they're lying.*

Later, as I thought about this whole episode, it wasn't that black and white in how my becoming the star witness happened or how my brain began to lie to me. Something instinctual forced me to agree to what he was saying. I blacked out whole portions of what he did, sending it to a place in me a million miles away. I embraced the lie that he was innocent, and convinced myself that I had to protect him.

I almost nodded to my dad but forced my gaze to Larry as he ambled toward me. I had to state my name and how I was related to John Butler. The word *daughter* almost lodged in my throat. When I turned to say this to the jury, none would make eye contact with me. It seemed as if there were many other interesting things besides me before them.

Larry took me through the allegations, and I made each one sound as innocent as my dad had persuaded me of. Yes, he was innocent. I could explain away each episode, even the ones I couldn't remember because they were black holes in my memory. But I'd try to be a good person for a change and be a loyal daughter to my innocent father.

At the end, Larry winked at me and smiled approvingly. He sat down and announced he was done.

The prosecutor, a man in his forties, trim and wearing glasses, stood and approached me. His attack came immediately. "Jenni, does your father hit you?"

My dad didn't do anything wrong. It was my duty to protect him. "Hit me?"

"Yes." The prosecutor waved his hand around in a flourish. "Yes. Punch you."

"Um, I'm not sure what you mean."

The prosecutor eyed me. "Didn't you tell the social worker who visited you at school, Sandra Branson, that your father beat you?"

I refused to look at my dad. I was sure he was staring at me. Now he knew that I had told. But I was going to somehow redeem myself from betraying him. "Yes, but I'm sure I deserved it."

The prosecutor's eyebrows raised. "Deserved it?"

"Yes." I nodded quickly. "I talk back a lot. If I were my dad, I'd punch me too."

The prosecutor stood fixated on me for a moment, clearly not expecting me to say that. "Okay. Let's talk about the night when Darla Benton stayed over. Do you remember that night?"

"I don't know. I remember lots of nights when she came over." My mind was trying to figure out what he was going to ask me.

"In the middle of the night, didn't your father come into the room where you both slept and start to rape her with you in the bed?"

My hearing became muted, and I blinked. *Did he? Oh God, I don't remember that.* I thought hard and tried to remember every time she had been over. Since I couldn't remember it, I said, "No. That didn't happen." *Had it?* My thoughts began to go up in flames. Something was lurking in the back of my head, asking for me to see it. I turned away, whether by choice or survival I wasn't sure.

"Isn't it true that you woke up to discover your father raping her and that he back-handed you to keep you quiet while he raped her. All the while she was begging for help?"

Had I? Had he? I didn't know. I honestly couldn't remember. The air became thicker and my vision got a little wonky. If I was honest with everyone including myself, I could say I had black spots in my memory that I couldn't force myself to remember. But to admit that meant I had to admit the possibility of that happening. So I pushed it aside.

That doesn't mean anything, I reassured myself. *Sit up straight and pretend to be confident.*

My dad's voice echoed in my head again, proclaiming his innocence.

"No, that isn't true." But I honestly didn't know. My heart was pounding loudly in my ears.

"Your father never raped her?"

"No." *Maybe. God, I don't know. I don't remember. Am I crazy?*

The questions went on and on, with me and the prosecutor in a dramatic dance, step and counter-step. I tried to be as thorough and honest as I could. As honest as the survival's denial and confusion would allow me.

Eventually, the questions stopped and I was dismissed. As I walked out, I looked over at my dad. He was busy writing and didn't even spare me a glance as I left the room. His disapproval came by denying me his eyes.

I went back to the witness room and waited. The small group of defense witnesses did everything we could to pass the time. We played paper football across the table, and talked about movies and anything that would distract us from the fact that we were waiting on twelve people to hear all of the testimonies.

Finally, the trial was over, and the jury had the case. We left the courthouse under a darker cloud than when we had gone in. It took them the evening to deliberate and to pronounce the verdict. Guilty. Not of all he was accused of, but guilty just the same. It was whittled down to two girls. One was an absolute verdict of rape, and the other of sodomy.

It was as if someone took a shotgun and blew part of my head off. Nothing was real, nothing was right. I couldn't find my footing in my own life. I was relieved and guilt-ridden at the same time. How did I reconcile my relief at never having to go back to a hell that was worse than the things he was accused of and yet, at the same time, ensure the blackest guilt over feeling like I betrayed my parent? No one helped me navigate it or understand where I was. I sunk into a repression of the events, self-loathing, and an even greater lack of desire to live.

I wished God would kill me. It seemed a just punishment.

CHAPTER 7

saved

A new neighbor moved into the townhouse next to ours and ended up being a sweet woman with three kids and a quiet husband. Sami went to church faithfully, and I was fascinated with her kind nature and patience, and how she seemed unflappable no matter what was going on. Not to mention she never wore a pair of pants and neither did her girls. They always wore the neatest skirts, because "that's what a woman wears."

She became fast friends with Emma, sharing sweet tea and laughs at our kitchen table. Emma bloomed in that friendship, and it intrigued me. Then Sami began to bring over her Bible and talk to Emma about God and how he had a plan for our lives.

I would listen, and as much as I loved Sami, I seriously doubted what had happened to me had any part of God in it. With clenched fists, I'd walk away and try to ignore what she was implying. To me, God was the crucifix under my pillow when I was a little girl. The one I clung to and begged to save me. God was on the cross and nowhere near my life.

I saw God as a god of retribution—who stood on ceremony, who was represented to my dad through crucifixes and relics. As much as I knew my dad was crazy, his notions about secret messages in the Bible and his interpretation stayed with me. I wasn't sure what to think about

God. I believed in him, sure. He walked around up in the heavens like an uninterested spirit unless you did something wrong or forgot to do the sign of the cross right. In my head, I was screaming "No, thank you!" All of my granny's teachings about God had been run over by my dad's interpretation.

One evening I was lounging on the couch watching TV when Emma came bursting through the door. "Jenni, I got saved tonight!" she exclaimed with a face that radiated. "I'm born again!"

I frowned and got up. "Well, keep that away from me," I said, heading for the stairs.

"You need to be saved too, Jenni."

"No, what I need is to go upstairs and get away from you. Leave me alone."

"Well, you will be going to church with us," she declared as Richard came inside with Henry.

I turned to her. "No, I won't."

"Yes, you will. If you live in my house, you will go to church."

I bit my lip. *If I lived in her house.* Great. Just great. I stared down at the beige carpet and considered my options. "Fine." *No way in hell am I going to church.*

I stalked up the stairs to my room, slammed the door, and threw myself on my bed. With a pillow held over my face, I screamed into it as loud as I could.

A few days later, that was put to the test when a knock sounded on my bedroom door on Sunday morning. "Jenni, you about ready?"

"For what?" I asked, barely awake.

"Church. Get dressed. We leave in ten minutes." Moments later, I heard her footsteps on the stairs.

I jumped out of bed, tore open my door, and followed. "I'm not going."

Emma sat on the couch, holding clothes for Henry. Wrangling his little body to herself, she began the process of getting him dressed as he struggled.

"Yes, you are," Richard said from behind me. "Hurry. Go get ready."

"I don't want to go!" I protested as he brushed past me.

"You're going. End of story." The look in his eyes told me I had no choice.

I clenched my fists and pounded up the stairs, muttering obscenities as I went. I changed into a t-shirt with a skull on it, dirty shorts and sneakers. I barely brushed my hair and left my smeared make up on my face. If she wanted me to go, she couldn't force me to look nice.

When I appeared at the front door ready to leave, Emma and Richard both gaped at me. After a moment Emma flashed a smile and headed for the car. Apparently the unsaved could dress however they wanted.

"Let's go," Richard said, standing by the door waiting for me to walk through.

I rushed out to the car and dove into the backseat, fuming. This was uncalled for.

The whole way there I picked at my cuticles, trying to block out the flood of Southern Gospel that came from the radio. This was going to end badly for them. They were making me go, but they couldn't make me participate.

When we walked into the tiny makeshift church that used to be a chicken coop. I sat in the very last row of seats, as far away from the preaching as possible. Emma frowned at me but didn't demand I move. Once she got passed me, I lay down across the seats, folded my arms over my chest, and closed my eyes, ignoring the bite of the chairs in my back.

I tried to go to sleep, but I couldn't block out the happy singing and wailed jubilation that came from the front. Then, the preaching was hellfire and brimstone, just loud enough to keep me from really dozing. When it was over and Emma came back down the row, she frowned at me.

I stood and adjusted my clothes. "Nice service," I spat and brushed past her to the car.

This went on for weeks—their insisting I go and my lying down and trying to sleep. We were at an impasse. Eventually Emma wanted to visit a church near where I used to live as a kid. It was a Pentecostal church but was supposedly pastored by a guy no older than twenty-one.

The church was small but felt relatively warm, with long rows of padded seats and a lot of younger people. I took the same seat in the back, but didn't lie down.

A short guy who appeared no older than seventeen approached, his eyes twinkling, and shook my hand. "Hi, I'm the pastor here."

This was the twenty-one-year-old pastor in question. "I'm Jenni," I said.

His small hand shook mine confidently.

Emma joined us. "Pastor, this is my cousin, the one I was telling you about."

"Ah." He nodded.

I frowned. I was the topic of conversation? Really? I shot Emma a hateful glance.

"Glad you could come, Jenni. Hope you enjoy the service." He offered a smile to Emma and walked away.

Emma didn't glance my way before she went up front to sit with Richard.

Good thing. I might have stuck my tongue out at her—or worse.

The service started with gospel singing. I hated Southern Gospel. It was too much like country for me. I tilted my head back and closed my eyes. If only I could push the activity around me out of my brain. Then, the pastor stood up and began to preach. I had heard sermons before, so this was nothing new. Typically, they were hellfire and brimstone. Get saved or you'll burn in hell. Well, I was in hell most days, so the warning didn't even faze me. But he did say one sentence that had me sitting up in my seat.

"I want you all to know God loves you very much. No matter what you've done, no matter where you are in your life, no matter the sin you've committed. God. Loves. You. If you ask him into your heart, he will forgive you and you will be a new creation in his eyes. Your past will be washed away in his love and forgiveness."

I blinked, thinking about this. God loved me? Jenni. Daughter of the monster. That couldn't be true, could it? The God who made the stars and the blades of grass I loved to run in as a little girl, loved me? My hands began to shake, and I looked down. I couldn't breathe.

God loves me? What?

The young pastor calmly declared, "You need only to respond to his call by walking forward and accepting him."

I fought back tears as my heart pounded in my ears. My feet wanted to start walking. But I sat there, engaged in a silent war. If I stood up, everyone would know how bad I really was. But God loved me, the pastor had said so.

It was compulsion and desperation. I jumped up before I could second-guess it and almost ran up front. I dropped to my knees and closed my eyes. *God, I hope you really love me. Because very few people do. I hope my dad's stuff doesn't matter. If you love me, then I give you my life.*

Something broke deep within me. The realization of love from something so much bigger than myself overwhelmed me, along with the sorrow over my dad, the trial, and my life. The crying wracked my body, and I kept my head down. I couldn't look at anyone.

A hand brushed the back of my head as a soft voice whispered in my ear, "Jenni, he accepts you. All of you. He loves every part of who you are and will forever." It was the young pastor.

We stayed like that for what seemed like hours, with me weeping and him stroking my hair. My gasps were the unformed words that I meant, that I would run after who God is if he'd have me. Even if I was the daughter of the monster.

part two

CHAPTER 8

shift

Years later, well into adulthood
Therapist office

"So, I'm glad to meet you. Where would you like to start?" The counselor sat back in her bright orange chair, her wavy dark hair framing her face. Her expression held a gentle smile with keen interest.

I sat back and reached for the pillow beside me to create a buffer between us. Or maybe it was self-soothing, I wasn't sure. But it felt good to hold it. "Um. I can't deal with my life anymore. I told my husband I was afraid I'd hurt myself." I stole a glance at her to see if her expression changed in anyway. It hadn't.

She seemed to wait on me to continue, and when I didn't, she spoke. "Why would you want to hurt yourself?"

The silence in the room belied the furious war of thoughts in my head. If I admitted what I really thought just about almost every second of the day, she'd commit me involuntarily and that felt like too much loss of control in this immediate moment. I need to hedge. "I have no purpose for being alive. Everyone would be better off if I was dead."

Had I really said that? Yes, I had. I'd opened an envelope to share parts of a dark letter I always carried inside. A letter that had so much dirt and filth on it.

I hadn't told anyone about my perfect plan for how I would end it all. I had bought a beautiful white eyelet lace gown that felt too nice to wear for everyday life. It was a special-occasion type of thing. My special occasion was dying. My plan was to rent a motel room, put on the gown, take every pill I had, and drift off into nothingness. I would leave a perfect corpse. It was a grotesque plan. Something kept me from carrying it out, but it was my ever-present option as an out if things got to be too much. Still, I couldn't share that with this nice lady before me.

The counselor let out a soft breath. "Why do you think everyone would be better off if you were dead?"

I shrugged as my eyes searched the floor for an executable response. Did I tell the truth, or did I lie? After all, only a few days prior I had sat in the car with my husband, Bill, telling him to take me to the hospital for fear I was going to harm myself. I was terrified of the way that suicide seemed like an intoxicating solution to pain I could no longer bear. He held me and got me through the night, then pushed me to seek counseling. Now I was a bit calmer but still a wrecked mess.

I stared down at the carpet. It was shag. Was that what they called it? Shag? Or Berber? How many variations of carpet were there?

"Jenni?"

I looked up to see the counselor waiting on me. I played dumb. "Huh?"

"Why do you think everyone would be better off if you were dead?"

"I just do."

She shifted in her chair. "How do you think your husband would feel about that?"

How would he feel? I knew how he'd feel. Horrible, distraught, forlorn. As much as I didn't want to hurt him, my pain was so much bigger than anything in my life. My pain told me I was worthless and that if I died, Bill would move on to someone better. That he deserved better than me.

As I sat there on that couch, the flow of my emotional bleed sped up. I couldn't look at her, and with each question she asked I avoided her eyes.

"Tell me about your mom and dad." The counselor's voice was

kind, even, with never any change in timbre. She was a disarming woman who seemed sincerely concerned for me.

There it was, the filth running all over me again. Where did I begin? So I tried to start from the beginning.

❀

As a child, I didn't know that my dad was mentally ill. I never heard the words *schizophrenic* or *paranoia* or anything that even resembled that. People deemed him "difficult," a "hot-head," and "odd," but never mentally ill. His diagnosis happened away from the spotlight of Collins and then evaporated like a bad dream in the morning light.

He was trim and stocky with dark hair, intense brown eyes, and fair skin. When he entered a situation, the air seemed to shift. Authority arrived, and people knew to submit to his orders without question. He rarely laughed, but when he did, it pierced the air in strong, short bursts.

While I loved my dad, I avoided him as well. Strangely, I wanted his attention and loathed it at the same time. I didn't understand his illness, so I found ways to turn his actions inward, believing I caused his violent outbursts. After all, my dad's knowledge and authority ruled our home. He knew the secrets of the universe and understood great mysteries in the Bible that no one else did—or so he said.

In contrast, my mom was stoic and unemotional. She had a robust figure, sandy-blond hair, and discerning bluish-green eyes. Little cracked the shell of her controlled essence, not even my attempts at affection, which she mostly rebuffed. We did share moments of playing records together and brushing her hair. Her ability to cope with my dad seemed to come from being unmoved by whatever war he engaged in. She was the icy contrast to his fire.

My childhood started in the bucolic hills of southeastern Kentucky in the small town of Collins. My mom's family owned a small patch of flat farmland at the base of forested hills marred with hardened, shell-rock trails. A weathered barn sat on the edge of the field with a small creek running behind it.

Each spring's arrival breathed magic over the land, awakening the fields and woods to glorious life—fragile wildflowers and new blades of grass escaped through the thick blanket of dead weeds like determined soldiers. The once-frozen creek flowed free with a gurgle of delight while birds chirped as they dove and chased each other against the clear blue sky.

New life brought relief to my eager mind. Winter dissolved, along with the suffocation of being inside with no escape. Now I was free to run and take deep breaths of the flower-scented air and bask in the golden warmth of the sun. I'd race off to the barn and look for mother birds building their nests high in the beams of the loft.

One spring when I was six my dad decided he wanted to breed dogs and bought a German Shepard named Smokey—a beautiful small female, ochre brown and black, probably not more than a few years old. We immediately took to each other. But while I considered her more than a pet, my dad saw her as a means to an end. He made a spot for her down in the barn and eventually bred her. Before long, Smokey began to swell with the promise of new life, and joy intoxicated me at the prospect of puppies. I would drift off to sleep at night counting potential puppies in my head and what names I would give them.

One evening, my dad announced that Smokey was in labor. I skipped along beside him as he ambled to the barn. Thick hay blanketed the floor of Smokey's stall as she lay on her side panting. After rushing to her, I knelt down and tried to soothe her by petting her fur.

"Stand over there!" he yelled.

Startled, I pushed my back flat against the rough wood of the barn wall, fearful to even move.

As time passed, I watched with wide eyes as large beans with legs seemed to come out of her. They didn't look more like puppies until Smokey licked them clean, and then they whimpered as they tried to move. Smokey nudged them with her nose until they found their way to her nipples.

Then my dad stepped in, and holding a cloth sack in one hand, he lifted the puppies to examine each one and proceeded to place some in the bag while placing others back at Smokey's side. "Females will be harder to sell," he said. "No one wants a dog that can get pregnant and have puppies." He bent over and tied off the bag with a string.

My heart started to pound. "What are you going to do?"

"Bury them," he said and headed for the door.

"No! Please don't!" I all but stumbled out after him.

My dad paused in the breezeway of the barn to retrieve a shovel, all the while ignoring my pleas. Little squeaks echoed from the bag that squirmed with little movements.

A few yards away from the barn, he dropped the sack and began digging a hole. I stood sobbing hysterically, begging for him to stop. My puppies! My beautiful little puppies! Daddy was going to bury them in a hole and they wouldn't be able to breathe!

"You idiot! If you don't go back to the house right now, I will beat you within an inch of your life!" he snarled.

At first I didn't move, but after he threatened to take off his belt, I obeyed, barely able to see through tear-blurred eyes. As I went in the back door, still sobbing, Mom rushed into the small kitchen.

"Please, Mom. Please go make him stop!" I begged, hardly able to breathe.

She waved me off but strained to see out the window. Her body then relaxed and she turned to the doorway.

There stood my dad, red-faced. "Stop your crying!" he demanded, and when I didn't, he pulled off his belt. A moment later, he began to swing.

When my dad whipped me, he didn't care where the belt landed, and his slaps were full force. Each slap ripped at my skin, and I raised my arms trying to counter the strikes—unsuccessfully. Even so, I kept begging him to dig up the puppies. He rose to his full height, heaving in air as he glared down at me. Tight-lipped, he rushed to his bedroom and slammed the door.

I ached, parts of me throbbing with physical pain while my heart grieved over the puppies. Mom tried to get me to stop crying, and when that didn't work, she sent me to bed early. All that evening and night, I sobbed and cried for my dad to go back and dig up the puppies. I could see them in my mind, little squeaking balls unable to breathe. Exhaustion finally won out and sleep took me.

The next morning, I immediately began begging and pleading for the lives of the puppies. Dad disgustedly slid his chair away from the table with a protesting squeak and got up, then walked out the door.

Following cautiously behind him, I watched as he pounded toward the barn. Hope bloomed within me when he grabbed the shovel and walked to the spot of the buried puppies. A heavy sigh released from my lips when, after digging for a short time, he lifted the soil-covered bag.

I dashed toward him, unafraid of any punishment I might get.

Pulling out the puppies, he lined them up side by side on the ground. Only a few moved slightly. The others lay still. Dad inspected each one, and once he sorted the living from the dead, he carried the live ones to Smokey.

I stood, fixated on the tiny, still bodies. Tears dropped off the end of my nose and landed beside them, a watery memorial of their too-short lives. "God, can you take them to heaven, please?" I whispered. Did puppies go to heaven? God seemed nice enough, so surely he'd do that, right?

"Go to the house," Dad ordered as he began to bury the dead ones.

Reluctantly I moved toward the house, but my gaze never left the spot where they lay, until I was inside. I cried for days over those lost little souls.

While the fate of the puppies followed me, my summer moved on. Days revolved around hide and seek with neighbor kids, building hay-bale houses in the barn loft, and catching slippery multi-colored salamanders in the creek behind the barn. We'd race through the fields adorned with Queen Anne's lace and red clover, to see who could claim fastest runner in the neighborhood. Only those who went barefoot had a chance to win. We marked time by climbing trees, making mud pies, making ink from pokeberry bushes, chewing wild mint, and sucking sweet nectar from honeysuckles.

When the air would cool over the field with the fading light, I had no choice but go inside, which meant being trapped in the house with my dad. I never knew what kind of mood he would be in, or what delusions or secrets he would find in the most common things. I treaded lightly and tried not to worry him, otherwise I might feel the belt.

One evening, I was playing tag in the yard with a boy who lived across the road. I ran as hard as I could, ducking through trees and other obstacles as I struggled to keep my pants—newly handed down from cousins—from slipping off my skinny waist. As I rounded the smoke-house, which sat between our small house and the garage that had been converted into my dad's shop, I spotted my mom.

"Where's your father?" she asked, looking confused.

I stopped.

Her concerned eyes searched around, her hands on her hips. "John?" she yelled toward the barn.

No reply came.

She shook her head with a sigh and went into the house, mumbling under her breath.

Before long, Mom yelled to me to come inside and get cleaned up for dinner. She lingered on the side porch, looking around, while I rushed past her. There was still no sign of my dad, but I wasn't worried. He'd appear sooner or later.

Mom and I ate supper in silence, and she kept checking the window, no doubt searching for Dad.

Suddenly, he appeared at the back door. With hay sticking out of his hair making him look like a deranged scarecrow, he began to babble. "The aliens came to see me," he told my mom with wild eyes and slurred words. "They want to take us away."

She shook her head. "John, what are you talking about? What did you take?"

He grabbed her arms. "We have to go! We have to hide. The aliens are coming!"

Mom jerked out of his arms, her eyes wide. "What are you talking about?"

"They are going to kill us all!" He rushed to the kitchen window. "The aliens are coming. I need my gun!"

"Keep your dad occupied," she ordered me, then covertly called the police as I stepped into his path to get his attention.

I asked him any question I could think of. What did the aliens look like? Where were they? When he would get distracted, I would pat his chest to get his attention.

Dad sat down in the middle of the dining room, appearing unable to keep himself upright. Banging of drawers pounded in the other room. I later learned that Mom was hiding all of his guns. I shiver now thinking what could have happened if he'd found them before she had.

My brain whirled, wondering if the aliens were coming or not. That was what he'd said, so shouldn't we go hide? And why did Mom want Dad to lie down? What was wrong with him?

"Stay down!" she yelled as she rushed over to Dad, fighting his attempt to get up.

He batted at her hands with a sloppy effort.

Mom leaned over him with all her weight and pushed him back down. She motioned for me to sit on him. I plopped my little body on his chest, trying to help.

Sirens bellowed in the distance, getting louder by the moment.

As my dad struggled, he screamed, "I went to heaven and they kicked me out, so I went to hell and have been with Satan!"

Tremors rattled me as I considered it. I couldn't breathe. Aliens... and now Satan.

Shouting men burst into the room wearing dark jackets and carrying bags. After pushing me aside, they attempted to get my dad under control so they could begin the process of taking him out to an awaiting ambulance. But my dad didn't make it easy, having landed a few punches and screaming obscenities.

My Dad's parents arrived but it took a moment for them to realize what was happening. As my papaw pushed further into the room with my granny on his heels, a look of horror crossed his face as he took in what was happening. "Johnny! Calm down!" he demanded at seeing all the commotion.

"Take Jenny with you," my mother told them. "I'm going with John."

The men loaded him into the ambulance and sped away as I watched alongside my grandparents. The vehicle got smaller and smaller, and the wails of the siren faded the farther down the road it got. Eventually my papaw's hand urged me toward the backseat of his car.

I pressed my face against the cold glass, watching as the indistinct landscape rushed by in monstrous shapes fashioned by oncoming night. Fear thrummed through me like bursts of lightening. I couldn't process it all. Aliens were going to come and get me, and my dad couldn't protect me because they took him away.

Later that evening, my grandparents put me in a bed in the back room of their house. I sat up and stared into the inky darkness, listening to the muted weeping of my papaw in the other bedroom. "That poor baby in there. What's going to happen to her?" he asked as his voice broke.

My granny's reply was so soft I couldn't hear it.

I played that question over and over in my head as fear stalked me like a wild animal. My hands trembled as my insides quaked. Death was coming for all of us, and we had nowhere to hide. Desperation wanted me to go to my papaw and crawl into his arms and have him hold me close. Instead, I sat frozen in place, staring at the ham radio on the desk by the bed. I knew that radio could talk to people far away. Maybe I could use it to talk to God, and he could come and save us all. Maybe God could stop my papaw from crying.

Pornography came into my life at age seven, around the time that I learned to masturbate. I'm guessing the porn came before me acting out, but that time is sort of blurry. What I've come to understand now is adults sharing pornography with children is sexual abuse, much like verbal abuse is still abuse -- it wounds and tears down a person. That is the way pornography was for me. Abuse. I encountered it in two places. At my home and from a cousin's house up the street.

It started with an evening when my parents left me alone at the house. My stepmom's younger sister was tasked with checking in on me periodically. With my parents gone I decided to look the closet that belonged to my them.

There were stacks of glossy magazines that had women with all their clothing off. Some were even bound and gagged. I couldn't process what I was seeing or how my body felt looking at that. In my mind, a trap door beneath me dropped and fell through, not really knowing how to climb back out at seeing those images. I was appalled, I was curious, but intrigued. I couldn't escape the discovery of what my parents looked at. I saw that they images related to the genitals and how people "touched" each other there.

A few days later I could begin going up the street to play with a cousin my age named Marvin. When I went into his family's trailer, I discovered the same types of magazines lying all around their house. While my eyes would try to avoid it, I was intensely curious. Marvin's parents weren't concerned with us looking at it. The pornography was everywhere, on the coffee table, in the bathroom and stacked on the small ledge between the living room and the kitchen. Marvin's dad would smile at me when I would look at it, like it was funny.

Once Marvin and I went to his room and I began to show him how to tie me up in his closet like I had seen in my father's magazines. He tried to do it right, but about that time his dad walked in. His dad loomed over me, larger than life with that same smile and that is where the memory ends. I have no idea what happened after that. It eats at me that I don't but the memory hovers on the edge of my awareness and I know that something bad happened.

A sickly patchwork blue and rust mobile home sat next to my friend's house and as kids we would play in it. It was riddled with porn of all kinds too - cartoons and playboy magazines. In retrospect, I didn't understand my body's reactions, I didn't understand what sex really was and the filter of it was confusing.

The wound was inflicted, and I was a changed child.

Life resumed into a blur of school, home, playing outside in the barn, and sleep. However, routine for me didn't last long. It seemed that things were always changing.

One such time, my dad came home on a Saturday morning with one hundred baby chicks in boxes stacked in the back of his van. I leaned in and watched as he carried one box after another down to the barn and placed them in a closed off area that used to be a pig pen that opened up to the outside yard surrounded with delicate fine-wired fencing. As he opened each box's lid, chicks ran out in a panic.

I jumped up and down, squealing because we had these beautiful fuzzy, little chicks that ran along the ground seemingly at the speed of light. There were so many of them that the ground appeared to be a blanket of yellow. Their non-stop chirping filled the air. I loved to walk in between them to catch them, but they were much faster than I was. They were my new little friends.

Two days later, my dad burst into the house early in the morning and pounded his way to his bedroom closet. After pulling out one of his guns, he started for the door. "Dogs dug under the fence and killed them all!" he bellowed to my mom as he disappeared outside.

My heart hammered at the thoughts of what might have happened. I could see my dad's tense frame heading for the barn. I followed him, realizing that little sound came from the chicken yard.

Getting closer, I saw tiny mounds of yellow speckled with spots of red lying in unnatural broken positions. Crushed heads and mangled bodies. A few were still alive, chirping for dear life.

I fell to my knees in the mud outside the fence and cried. Almost all of my babies were dead. Suddenly a gunshot rang out from the barn. I ran to the breezeway of the barn to see my dad raise the gun again, pointing at something in the corner, and pull the trigger.

Bang!

I screamed.

He turned toward me. "Get in the house, stupid!"

My legs carried me away as more gunshots echoed.

I rushed through the screen door and back to the bedroom window to watch my dad as he carried his gun into the woods. He whistled to the unseen dogs, and they responded, appearing eager to meet him. Without hesitation, he lifted the gun and began shooting.

Tears rushed down my face as I thought about the dogs and my chicks. Of course, the dogs had killed my chicks, but I didn't want them dead too. Couldn't we just be angry at them and not hurt them? Apparently not.

"You're just too soft-hearted," Mom said as she walked into the room. "Those dogs had it coming. So quit crying."

As she left, shame filled me because I wasn't stronger, wasn't tougher. I knew my mom didn't approve of tears. Her family upbringing had taught her that emotions were weakness. Her children would be strong, she'd make sure. While I believe she tried her best to raise her children with what she knew, her distain for emotion and tears translated into dislike of that part of me—that she disliked me. So I tried with everything in me to be stronger, to not feel, to push down any sadness. But it felt like trying not to breathe, and I just couldn't do it.

For years after that, whenever I had to go to the barn, I would avoid the corner of the stairs leading up the loft that had a deep-red blood stain, the grim evidence that a dog had died there. I didn't want to face that.

A month later, my dad bought a new batch of chickens, although not as many as before. Taking precautions to keep any dogs out, he placed large rocks around the chicken wire to fortify the soft ground.

The chicks grew, and my summer was filled with playing with our rooster, Big Ben, and collecting eggs from the hen house. Of course, I had to be alert to avoid the hens attempting to scratch me. No matter how fierce the hens were in those moments, I still loved them and gave them all names.

At the end of that summer, my dad called me out behind his shop. There he sat by a stump, an ax in one hand and Big Ben dangling from his feet, flailing and squawking. "I want to teach you something," he said. Then he laid Ben on the stump and brought the ax down on his neck. The *thud* hit me square in the chest, and Ben's head landed in the spiny grass at the base of the stump.

I felt the blood drain from my face.

My dad produced a knife and began to gut Ben and pull out parts of him. "You see," he began genteelly, "this is his heart. Oh, and these are the lungs." One by one, he made a biology lesson out of my pet, spreading his insides out for us to see.

I could only cry as he dismantled something I loved so dearly. That seemed to define Dad to a T—hacking good things into bloody, unrecognizable pieces.

I couldn't move when he took what remained of Ben into the house. He announced with a smile, "We are going to have some good fried chicken tonight."

What? Eat Ben?

Later, as I sat at the dining room table with puffy eyes red from sobbing, the chicken...Ben...lay in batter-fried pieces in front of me. My hands were frozen at my sides. How dare I eat something I loved so much?

I couldn't even begin to put that in my mouth. Eventually Mom relented and took the food away with a terse reprimand, then sent me to bed early without anything else to eat.

Throughout all the chaos, I discovered one thing that seemed to quiet my soul: telling stories. And not just telling them, but acting them out as if I were the characters. As it turned out, I had a gift for mimicking people.

At school, when the recess bell rang, I would bolt up and join the mass of children going outside to the playground. This was my time to be in front of my friends. At the edge of the soccer field at my Catholic school was a small rise of land. Taking my place at the bottom, I awaited my audience's arrival. Here I would pick up from a continuing story or start a new one. I was the performer in a world I could share with others.

My friends gathered around, and I took them on journeys to other places filled with magic and wonder. In my stories, the heroes always won, overcoming the worst circumstances. Sometimes I would take television shows and create new characters to assist the heroes in overcoming the adversity in their lives. Sometimes I would interject myself into them, even if I gave myself a different name. Then, like a queen in her court, I would share the stories with my friends like a theatre performer.

Stories became my escape. If the real world was broken around me, my make-believe world would always make it right. An odd sort of theme developed in all of my stories that I didn't share with my friends. Somehow, I became the hero's daughter and he loved me. We'd go off and fight the evil force together. But in the end, I would always return to my existence as an idiot, emotional girl who could never get the approval of either parent.

My heart was pounding. I had told my counselor more than I had ever intended. I wasn't sure how my childhood had anything to do with now. Nevertheless I had shared things with her that I wasn't even sure mattered. Maybe they did.

CHAPTER 9

burning down my life

I stared at my feet, but I could tell my counselor hadn't moved an inch. She didn't even write. Weren't they supposed to do that? She never did.

"Sounds like lots of chaos in your house," she breathed.

Chaos.

Yes.

Yes, lots of chaos.

I nodded and threw in a noncommittal shrug to somehow make light of the fact that I was terrified of my dad daily and desperately wanted the love of my mother. Even then, there was my stepmom and my birth mother, two who seemed emotionally out of reach.

"You didn't feel safe, did you?"

How did you guess? My eyes lifted to hers as they filled with tears. I wiped them away, embarrassed by my weakness. My emotional weakness. "No, I never felt safe."

As a little girl, I barely slept for fear of what was in the dark. My dad had talked so much of demons and how he talked to them, that I slept with a cross under my pillow that I had gotten for first holy communion. The blankets offered me a little comfort even though I would arrange them tightly around myself so nothing could get to me. But then the dark would fade, and day would dawn and a new type of trying to find my own comfort came. But there wasn't much I could do. I just tried not to get in the way or need too much.

"You haven't told me much about your mom," she prodded.

"Well, the woman I told you about was my stepmom, really. My birth mother left when I was fourteen months old."

My counselor pressed her lips together for a slight moment, an indication that she didn't approve of my birth mother doing that any more than I did.

"I was nine when I learned about her. She just pulled up and introduced herself. 'So, hey there, I'm your mom. See you later,' just like that."

"Was that confusing?"

Confusing? "Oh, yes."

I dangled upside down from the tree in the front yard as a car pulled up our gravel driveway. No movement came from the idling car.

Strange. Why isn't anyone getting out?

I dropped from the tree and started toward the car and stopped at the edge of the gravel. The sharp sun beat down on me while a trickle of sweat ran down my back. I stood there grinning, waiting to be the one who greeted the customers.

My dad's small shop was nestled in what had been a garage. Folks frequently pulled up to see him about the repair of televisions, radios, and anything electronic, which he could fix with ease. He'd had a gifting with gadgets from the time he was a small boy. One time he had even shown us a newspaper article written about him when he was nine, showcasing his uncanny ability. The article had pronounced him as a genius of sorts, being able to unravel all the secrets of electronics. After serving four years in the navy, his gifting became more honed and turned into a small business. He fixed anything and everything that was juiced by electricity. He would later attempt to patent some inventions but with little success.

As I inched closer to the passenger side, a woman with glasses and curly short hair shaped like a helmet smiled at me and cranked down the window. "Hello there," she breathed.

"Hi," I said eagerly, standing barefoot on the gravel as it bit into the bottom of my feet. "Are you here to see my dad?"

She frowned slightly and shook her head. "No, Jenny," she replied sweetly, "we're here to see you."

The smile slid off my face as if melted by the heat. I scowled. "Me?"

"Yes, you," she confirmed and shifted in her protesting seat.

"Who are you?" I began to twist my fingers into my shirt as I took a small step back.

"Why, I'm your great aunt. This here beside me is your grandmother, and back here is your mother." She waved behind her.

My eyes slowly followed the motion. It took a moment to see through the glare on the rolled-up glass, but a woman sat in the back. I could see distinct bird-like features on a face with wide pale blue-green eyes. The woman gave me a slight smile and a little wave, but she never lowered her window.

I shook my head violently, stepping back again. "No, my mom is in the house."

The woman gave a patronizing look. "No, honey. That woman in there is not your mother. This is your mother," she insisted. "We came all this way to see you."

My heart began to beat wildly and my mouth went dry. "No. My mom is in the house." I glanced over my shoulder right as my mom appeared at the storm door. As she opened it, I heard the car gears engage, then the back tires spun in an effort to find purchase on the gravel. I jerked my head around as they backed out of the driveway and then sped down the road.

My heart was loud in my ears. I shook my head in disbelief and strolled to the house.

My mom held the door open for me.

"Can you believe it? That weird lady said she was my mother." I laughed at how absurd the whole thing was. What kind of customer would say they were your mom?

Mom pulled me into the house with a little tug as my dad appeared from the back room.

89

Upon seeing Mom's face he stopped, his brows coming down hard. "What?"

"A woman pulled up and said the lady in the backseat of the car was my mother," I told him.

His eyes flicked from mine to my mom's. She must have confirmed it because he gave a slight nod and sighed. Putting his hands on his hips, he looked hard at me. "That was your mother."

Like a pane of glass struck by a pebble, a small crack started at the top of my soul.

"But she is a whore, been married to lots of men, and tried to kill you," he said as plainly as if he were describing what we were going to have for dinner.

I blinked once, again and then again. The crack rushed down my insides. "What?" I barely forced out and pointed. "Isn't she my mom?" My breathing was loud in my ears.

"No, your mother was in that car. But I saved you from her. She starved you and tried to kill you. She's a whore and mentally ill. Now go back outside."

I stood there as the crack shattered the glass of my soul, sending shards through me, cutting through the arteries of my identity. That had been my mother? But she was a whore? She tried to kill me? My *real* mom tried to kill me?

Rough hands turned me around and pushed me back outside to go play, but all I could do was wonder why I hadn't known. Surely if that woman had been my mother, she would have felt differently about me, right? Why hadn't I known who she was?

The thoughts of my mom in the kitchen not being my actual mom overwhelmed me, but on a certain level it made a little bit of sense. I had always felt like an outsider and never able to penetrate the wall she kept around her. I'd always wanted her to let me in, but maybe she couldn't completely accept me because I wasn't her own. I belonged to the woman racing off down the road. Maybe that was why my dad always said I was an idiot, because I belonged to a bad woman.

I ran to the road, gazing down to where I'd last seen the car, and a profound ache threatened to double me over. I wanted her to come back and get me—to save me from the hell I was in now. Maybe I could talk her into loving me? Maybe she could say she was sorry for trying to kill me, and maybe I could be lovable to her. Maybe, just maybe I could get her to love me, and I could be okay with her being a bad person.

The scent of mint wafted on the hot, humid air, and I returned to the cold stone slab of the front porch and sat down. I watched the end of the road for her return, all the while my mind engaging in the oddest war. If she was a whore and had tried to kill me and I wanted to be with her, what did that make me? Why did I want her so much? Did it make me a bad girl to want her as much as I did? It was possible she'd come back. After all, she had come for me this time, right? I wanted to talk to her, to prove to her she could love me. That I could be a good girl. She just had to come back.

For many weeks after, I would sit on the porch and wait for her. I would make sure I was ready for her to pull up so I could jump in her car and be taken away. But she never came back.

Even now, I think about how I ached that day. The deep longing for my mom and dad to hold and care for me, to create a place of safety for me. But I'd never felt safe. I simply learned to survive, but I never learned how not to long. The neediness never went away. I just learned to mask it.

I eventually quit waiting on the porch, but I could never rid myself of the sound of broken glass clinking inside me.

There were salamanders in the creek. My rapt attention was on the one I wanted to catch. I moved as slowly as I could, but no matter how I tried, the salamanders always saw me.

A sound caught my ear—someone yelling. I rose from the creek bed and started toward the house.

"I mean it!" my dad's voice bellowed as I got closer. "I will destroy everything you own!"

As I rounded the corner, my dad disappeared into the house.

I looked across the road to the long white ranch house that belonged to my step-grandparents. When my parents fought, my stepmom always retreated to her parents' house. When she did, she always left me, and it was another grim reminder that I wasn't hers. The rejection began to bite down hard. I shook my head and forced the walls up inside to hold myself together.

A flicker of movement caught my eye as my dad burst out onto the porch, breathing hard. His clinched hands had me sucking in a breath. When he was angry, people needed to hide or they would be hurt. "You better come back here right now!" he screamed in the direction of where my stepmom was hiding. He waited, his chest rising and falling.

Across the road, a curtain moved slightly in the window.

Dad turned and went back into the house.

I stepped inside and waited by the door. The sounds of destruction emanated from his and Mom's bedroom. Metal hangers clinked together, and then he bolted out of the room carrying a load of clothing. I could only stare as he walked out the front door.

Through the storm door's glass, I saw him drop them unceremoniously on the front lawn. He stormed back into the house with quick strides, then his flailing arms grabbed anything they could reach. Mom's hairdryer, her clothes—it didn't matter what it was. If anything was within his reach, he carried it out.

This time he didn't come back inside. Instead, he strode to the side of the house and returned with a bottle of lighter fluid. After squirting it over the items, he lit the mound on fire.

Brilliant flames engulfed the pile in a whoosh.

His face twisted into a mask of satisfied anger as he defiantly watched the house across the road. Finally, Dad came back into the house and paused to glare at me. "She's not your mom anymore."

This reminded me that I was, in fact, the daughter of a woman who wanted to kill me. A woman he saved me from. That the lady across the street who I desperately wanted to love me was not my real mom. I shouldn't have wanted to belong to her either, because she was apparently bad too.

"Okay," I said softly. But what did I call her? Her name was Kay. Did I call her that? "Kay," I said to myself, testing it on my lips. But it felt foreign.

Dad came back through the living room, and I realized he was carrying out the Christmas presents from their hiding place in the closet. My eyes fixated on an outfit I knew was mine. A primary-colored Crayola outfit with suspenders, an outfit I begged for. But like everything else around him, it was going to be a victim of my dad's temper.

I watched in horror as it was thrown onto the fire, along with other things. He was burning *Christmas presents*.

I decided to save something that had meaning to me. After rushing into their room, I grabbed the one thing that gave me a connection to Mom—or Kay. Hair rollers and a styling product called *Dippity-Do*, which Mom...Kay said helped my curls stay in after my hair dried overnight. If she was gone, wouldn't they be mine now? I didn't want my dad to burn them. I liked it when Kay rolled my hair. It felt like she cared. I would never let these go. Never.

My dad kept the fire burning, and soon sirens approached. But I sat, transfixed by the small items I'd saved. I wasn't going to watch whatever was happening outside. Eventually the yelling stopped and everything was quiet.

After an hour, Kay came back. Her footsteps in the hall sounded as if they paused at her bedroom, no doubt taking in all the damage. After a few moments she appeared in the doorway of my room.

I'm not sure why, but I whispered, "I don't have to call you Mom anymore."

Her eyes flickered, but she said nothing and walked away.

Why had I said that? I didn't know. It felt good to be defiant to her considering she didn't take me with her to Mamaw and Papaw's. *Wait, what do I call them now?*

Kay soon returned with outstretched hands. "Give those to me."

I stared at her. She wanted her things back, and I wanted what? Something I couldn't even name. Maybe there could be a trade. She was going to take back all the possibility in those seemingly insignificant things, and it broke my heart. Eventually I surrendered them and watched her walk out of the room again.

I would have done anything for her to sit down on my bed and pull me into her arms, to have her stroke my hair and reassure me that she loved me—to explain the day and to reassure me everything was okay. But she didn't. No one ever did.

Her bedroom door closed with a slight click.

I wasn't sure where my dad was, but he was gone for the rest of the evening.

Lying in the darkness with my clothes still on, I pulled up the covers and reached under the pillow, grabbing onto the crucifix as I cried.

God. Please come love me.

The tears flowed until I drifted off to sleep.

CHAPTER 10

Empty house

Tears ran down my face and dropped onto my hands like melted wax from a candle. My raw soul felt exposed to this stranger who sat patiently listening.

"That had to be pretty confusing," she said.

"My entire childhood was confusing." My thumb rubbed the palm of my hand, tracing the deep lines there. I wondered what someone would think if they could really interpret my life by those random folds.

"How do you feel about your stepmom now?"

I shrugged. "We get along now. We had a great talk not long after she married this really nice guy. He softened her quite a bit. She apologized to me."

"How did that feel?"

"Good. Validating. Late."

"Late?"

"Part of me wanted her so desperately when I was little. I would have done anything to have her love me. Instead, I always felt too needy, too emotional, too desperate for physical affection. I rarely got any. Even though I understand now that she told me that her family never showed emotion or affection because that was considered weakness, I still missed what she could never give."

"You sound like you were two very different people."

"We were—and are." I took in a deep breath and thought about that. I never felt good enough for Kay. Never. "Then when I was twelve, she was gone. She divorced my dad and left me there." My gut clenched at the memory.

At the end of my fifth-grade year, my parents built a house on the edge of town in a new subdivision. It sat up on a small ridge and had a sloped one-acre yard. As much as this was something to be excited about, I wasn't thrilled with leaving the creek and the barn that had been my haven in the midst of deep pain.

My first outing to see the new white house with black shutters was to spend the day picking up rocks in the yard. My dad was suddenly obsessed with having a perfect yard. So I would wander the yard and pick up any type of rock that seemed bigger than my hand and chuck it into the next lot while he was in the garage setting up his shop.

We were far away from my stepmother's family, and that felt isolating. But there were difficulties between Kay and my dad that I didn't see at the time, but at that point, everything was quiet. There were no episodes or craziness.

Not long after we moved in, Dad started throwing accusations at me. "Kay can't deal with you anymore. You're just too much, and you're not her kid." Then he would leave with Kay to go out to eat.

I watched as the car pulled away, dumbfounded.

This became the lie he threw at me day after day before he and Kay would go off to do things and leave me at home. I couldn't help whose daughter I was. I wanted to shed my skin, change my blood, anything to be included with them.

To the world, I was the spawn of John Butler, but to him I was the undesirable child of Rosa Lee. The recriminations were long and nothing I could change, but it painted a broad stroke of shame over me. It was a knife tearing through my gut when Dad and Kay would leave. The large house, the loneliness, and my self-hatred mocked me.

Toward the middle of my sixth-grade year, I came bounding off the school bus and walked home like any other day. As I stepped into the house, a grim feeling greeted me.

My dad sat at his desk in the living room, staring at the papers there, but didn't seem to notice me come in. I went back to my room to lay my book bag and coat on the bed. When I glanced across the hall to my parents' room, it looked like someone had torn through it.

I rushed back out to the living room. "Where's Mom?"

"She's gone, and it's all your fault."

The words hung in the air. I couldn't breathe. "She's gone?" I forced out. "Forever?"

"Yes," he bellowed. "You were just too much. Just like Rosa! I swear, living with you is like living with her! That whore!" With that, he scooted back so hard that his chair tipped over. His hands balled into fists as he glared at me.

Recoiling, I turned and ran to my room and slammed the door. *She has to take me with her*, was all I could think.

I snuck quietly out of my room and into my parents' room, then picked up the phone and dialed my mamaw's number, hoping that was where my mom was.

Mamaw sighed when I asked for her, and there was shuffling on the other end.

As soon as my mom got on the line, I began to plead. "Please, Mommy. Please come and get me. I want to be with you."

She sighed heavily. "I can't, Jenni. I just can't. You aren't mine. I don't have a legal claim to you. I'm sorry."

Tears ran down my face. "Please, Mommy. I'll be good and I won't talk much. I know you say I talk too much, but I promise to be quiet. Please."

Mom kept telling me she couldn't come and get me, and with a blunt, "I'm sorry, Jenni," she hung up the phone, leaving me grasping the receiver.

I went back to my room and threw myself onto the bed, then wrapped myself up in the covers, feeling abandoned. I kept thinking about how my birth mother had never come back and now my other mother was gone and I was left with the monster. It was unreal. I lay there all day and all night until I woke up to late-morning light.

I guess I'm not going to school today.

I was a nobody child, and a desperate need to belong and to be wanted clawed at me from the inside out, but no one wanted me. Not my father and not my mothers.

Days blended into a weird sort of anguish. Dad began to smoke pot and would sit in the living room showing me how to roll joints. Then he would smoke a whole bag of pot, mix it with alcohol and pills, and just lose his mind. His demons would come to life in stunning color, and he would roll around on the living room floor, out of his mind.

A few days after my mom left, I went to my parents' bedroom, got an alarm clock, and figured out how to make it work. Soon I was getting myself up and going to school. I learned to be even more quiet and blend into the wallpaper. When Dad was high or drunk, I knew where to hide in the basement.

"What about your birth mom?" the counselor asked. "Did she come around after that?"

I shook my head and pressed my lips tight. "Nope. I didn't see her again until I was in the sixth grade, and then it was only for about three days. My dad had called her. I still don't know why."

The school bus dropped me off at the end of our subdivision's road, and I ambled toward our house. After coming through the front door, I stopped short. A strange woman was sitting on our brown patchwork couch with my dad. Her dark hair hung long and thick down her back, and her eyes filled with tears when she saw me.

"Hello, baby," she whispered.

I immediately knew who she was—my birth mother. The mother I'd waited for every day for months, and now she was staring at me as she stood.

I touched her with a trembling hand.

She gave me a benevolent smile and took my hand. Her skin was warm. "I'm going to stay with you guys for a few days. Is that okay?" She waited, seeming to gauge my reaction.

I nodded as she pulled me to herself. She smelled like flowers.

When she pulled back, I blurted out, "Will you make cookies with me?"

Her eyebrows rose. "Cookies?"

"Yes, cookies." I wanted to tell her that was what I'd heard mothers did with their daughters. They made cookies. They made cookies and smiled at each other and loved each other. The cookies proved it, right?

She regarded me for a few moments, then said, "Of course I'll make cookies with you."

My heart danced! My real mom was going to bake cookies with me. That somehow gave me a little boost in value. It's hard to explain, but it seemed like affirmation to me and I couldn't wait.

My dad called her attention back to him, and she gave me a reassuring look as she turned away. I spent the day peeking around the corner at her from the hallway. I caught bits and pieces of the conversation. *Mortgage* and *foreclosure* were two words I didn't know, but I continued to listen.

That night, as my mom sat on the couch in the living room, I couldn't help staring at her. She'd cross her legs and laugh at something my dad said or would lean on her arm poised on top of her knee. Her voice was sweet, almost like a child's.

I glanced down at my own hands and wondered if I looked like her. My dad always reminded me that I did, but he'd always made it sound like that was a bad thing. Yet here she sat, talking with him like things were fine. Did she say she was sorry and now it was okay? Or was she going to leave again? I almost couldn't breathe at the thought. It seemed as if I made one wrong move, she would disappear again, and I wanted to be good so she'd stay.

My mom reached into her purse and pulled out a brush. As she stroked her hair, I kept thinking about how pretty she was. I wanted to have a reason to touch her.

"Can I brush your hair?" I whispered.

She paused, then smiled while holding out the brush. "Of course."

I wedged myself behind her on the couch and began to brush her thick mane. I don't know where I got the idea, but then I began to braid it. I wanted to see what it would look like on her head. With my fingers in her hair, I reveled in the fact that I was actually touching *my mother*. I wondered if she was going to stay forever.

My mind went back to when I would rub Kay's feet on this same couch. How I wanted to please her so she would love me, and it was reflected in the same motion of that brush through my birth mom's hair. Two women, two people I loved and wanted to love me back. Two women, two rejections, two messages of not being good enough. But I was going to prove I could be a good girl.

The next day I was allowed to stay home from school, and I was so excited I could hardly keep from bouncing around. My natural inclination was to talk a lot, and with my mom here, it became more pronounced. I talked to her about my dolls and playing outside, anything I could think of to keep her attention on me, and it seemed to work. She stayed focused on me and would periodically nod.

When evening came, my mom and dad went off to the store and returned with all the ingredients to make chocolate chip cookies. She and I set about making them, and I couldn't help but smile and feel an odd sense of affirmation. I was normal in that fleeting instance. It was one of the best moments of my life.

The following morning, I was sent to school, although I hated to leave my mom. I resisted the urge to cling to her when we hugged before I left. Throughout the day, I tried to focus on doing everything I needed to so I could return to her.

I had a mom.

I. Had. A. Mom!

My own mom who gave birth to me!

Eventually the school day was over, and I rushed to the bus. After getting off the bus, I ran the length of the road and burst into our house. Dropping everything by the door, I searched for her.

My dad seemed to ignore me as I rushed around.

I finally stopped in front of him. "Where's Mom?"

"She's gone," he said and let out a huff of cigarette smoke that billowed up to the ceiling.

Gone? My eyes began to fill with tears. "But...why?"

"She tried to poison my tea, so I threw her out." He took another huff off of the cigarette and shifted to cross his legs.

I blinked in horror. And then blinked again.

"She tried to kill you?" Surely this wasn't true. She'd made cookies with me. She let me brush her hair. Maybe he was wrong.

"Yes!" he screamed, his eyes alight with fury. "She tried to kill me, and she'll try to kill you too. So don't even mention her again! Do you understand?"

I nodded as all my hope ran out of me and puddled at my feet. My mom had tried to kill my dad. Maybe it was my fault. I could have told her that it was bad to do things like that. Maybe she didn't know. But people who tried to kill other people were bad, so she was bad? Nausea spread through me. I was her daughter, and that made me even worse than I already was.

"She's a whore!" he bellowed as he left the room.

I was motherless again. I curled up on my bed and cried myself to sleep.

I'd learn later that my dad had asked her to do some illegal things. When she refused, he threw her out and told her to never come back.

When I left the counselor's office, I felt as if I could breathe a little easier.

Bill sat in the car waiting for me. "So? How was it?" he asked when I got in.

"Okay, I guess. I like her. She lets me talk."

He smirked. "That's what she's supposed to do."

I scoffed. "I know that. But still, I didn't think she'd be that easy to talk to."

Reaching over, he squeezed my hand. "I'm glad. Are you going to see her again?"

I nodded. "Yes."

"Good." He put the car in drive.

As I lay in the darkness that evening with Bill softly snoring beside me, I let my tears flow. Thinking about Kay and Rosa had lanced me.

The same plaguing thoughts ate at me. I should be dead.

I just wished I had the nerve to actually do it.

CHAPTER 11

there goes normal

My insides twisted as I sat before my counselor. She smiled at me, but that did little to quell the riot taking place in my mind. A part of me screamed to keep quiet and another part waited for the ability to say things I had never told anyone.

"How was your week?"

"Okay, I guess."

I didn't want to get out of bed. Why am I even here?

She asked me what had caused me to feel so suicidal that I thought I might do myself harm.

The first thing that came to mind was a situation related to a church dissolving—a church at which I had felt really plugged in and like I was doing my "calling." When the church fell apart, so did my desire to live. Well, okay, the desire to live was tenuous at best. But "working" in the church had been mission, it had been purpose, and it had been my "good" identity. At church, I was good. Now that it was gone, I was back to being nothing, less than nothing, scum on someone's shoe. I was unimportant and fell apart.

I knew what I felt was crazy, that losing a role in a church made me suicidal and plunged me into the worst sort of darkness. But it had, or maybe it pulled out what was already there. I wasn't sure and was so exhausted by people telling me I was too emotional or just "mental."

The best part about counseling was that my counselor never seemed to judge me. Never. She was kind and warm, and seemed sincerely interested in what I had to say. Besides my husband, I felt like she was the first person who wanted to understand me. For her it was certainly to help me, but her care for me still bled through.

"Tell me what's on your mind."

I really felt at ease with my counselor, but on a different level I was afraid to say too much for fear she would reject me. Could I really tell her everything? She could stand up at any moment and tell me to see myself to the door. I know I certainly would tell me that.

I took in a deep breath and began.

Reprieve from home life came in the form of roller skating. There was nothing like gliding on the floor bathed in colored light while music played in pounding beats. Skating along with the wind against my face, losing myself for a few hours on Friday and Saturday nights, became what I lived for.

My dad didn't seem to care what I did at this point, so I would find my way to the skating rink and back. I would stand at the rink's front door and panhandle for the three dollars to get in to skate until ten, and if I was lucky, I could beg five and could stay until midnight. The owner of the skating rink got to know me and would endure me with stoic disapproval, but he never tried to stop me. At the end of the night, I didn't always have a way home and that was scary. I would wait out front and ask everyone until someone agreed to give me a ride.

One evening, a girl I barely knew said her mother would be willing to take me home. I was relieved that I'd be riding home with a woman and a girl and not squeezed in between guys. I slipped into the back of the warm car, and we pulled away from the lit parking lot. As we drifted down the road in the dark, the woman started talking to her daughter.

"How was your night?" she asked sweetly while adjusting the heat.

"It was okay," the girl replied. "Did Dad make it home?"

"Yep. He was sorry he missed you. He went to bed but wants to be woken up when you get home." She reached over and took her daughter's hand.

The girl smiled at her mom. "Okay. Good."

As they continued to chat, my eyes widened as a wild hunger scratched at my insides. This woman seemed to really love her daughter and wasn't put off by her. After all, she had actually picked her up to take her home with absolutely no ire. Whereas my mother had walked away from me three times without another word, this woman was driving in the dead of night to pick her daughter up from skating and talking to her like she mattered.

My hunger turned to profound jealousy as I watched them interact, thinking about how what I was witnessing was what normal was. Or rather, that it was what love was about. Part of me wanted to crawl over the seats and beg her to take me home, to adopt me as one of her own. Instead, I sat mesmerized at their interactions, fighting back the tears that threatened to come.

In that moment, whys began to rumble in my mind. Why had I been given the life I had? Why did I have the parents I had? Why couldn't life be normal? Why? Why? Why?

Asking that was like talking to the wind. Those things were carried off to silence and I'd be left in the ruin of my horrible life. Those whys led to the first seeds of thought of life not being worth living if it only consisted of what I had been given with my dad.

As we turned down the dark country road to my house, the car lights passed over my dad's van, which sat cock-eyed on the side of the road. The lights were on but it wasn't moving.

"Wait," I said suddenly. "That's my dad. You can let me out here."

"Are you sure?" she said. "I mean, it's late—"

"I'm sure. That's my dad."

She reluctantly pulled over, and I got out with a "thank you" and rushed to the van. As I opened the door, the heavy scent of alcohol drifted out and I knew I was in trouble. My dad sat in the driver's seat with his arm stretched out at his side and his head back on the headrest. Instinctively, I turned back to the car and watched the taillights move away down the road.

There goes normal, I thought, watching them drive away. My brain screamed at the unfairness of it all. But what could I do? I was Jenni Butler, and I couldn't change who I was any more than I could change my eye color. Turning back to my very abnormal life, I stepped up into the van. "Dad?" I said carefully and slid across the passenger seat. He was either drunk or high or both—I wasn't sure. I couldn't tell from moment to moment with him, so anything was possible.

His head jerked up and he met my gaze with a glazed, unfocused stare. "Oh. Jenni..."

I pulled the door shut. The interior light stayed on.

"Dad?" I said again, hoping to focus him. "We need to drive home."

With a flick of his fingers, he threw something small to me. I looked down to see I was holding a liquor bottle lid. "There," he sneered. "You're the devil. We're going to die!" Jerking the van into gear, his foot slammed down on the gas pedal as he threw his head back against the seat, unconcerned with what he was doing.

The van violently lurched forward toward a steep rock embankment along the road. At the speed we were going, we would surely crash and maybe die.

Instinctively, I jerked open the van door and jumped out, then landed hard in a hole. I sat upright to watch the van race toward the hillside. Before it hit, the van screeched to a stop.

In the darkness, beneath the star-laced sky and amid the soft sounds of tree frogs, the van sat with its lights flooding the side of the embankment with light, mere feet from making contact.

My breathing was loud in my ears as I listened against the night for some indication of what my dad was doing. Nothing moved. Sound seemed to be sucked up by the cool night air.

I couldn't move. My heart hammered so hard in my chest I thought it would explode.

After a few moments, the van was put into gear and it slowly turned to head down the road toward our house.

I didn't rush after it. Instead, I turned and ran the other way, not knowing what I was going to do. Pain radiated in my leg, and I realized I must have hurt it jumping into the hole.

Soon, I caught sight of the Wendy's restaurant lit up like a beacon of hope across the four-lane highway. I rushed across the lanes and walked in. The smell of hamburgers and cooking grease greeted me.

To my absolute horror, the Collins football team was all there, having just arrived back from an away game. They were in line to order. I kept my eyes forward, trying to ignore them as I approached the counter.

The boy behind the counter wore a rust-and-brown newsboy cap with wavy hair sticking out from underneath. He regarded me with wide eyes, glancing down at my leg and back up to my face.

My gaze followed his, and I saw a large bloody gash on my shin. I pushed that out of my mind, more concerned about other things. "Can I use your phone, please?" I asked as sweetly as I could. "I need to call…" —but who could I call?—"my granny to come get me."

He picked up the receiver with a look of distain and handed it to me.

I really had no idea how my granny was going to come get me since she didn't drive. But she was the only lifeline I had left. I needed to call her and hoped she could help me figure it out.

"What's the number?" he asked, a little annoyed, as his fingers hovered over the numbers to dial.

A hand rested on my shoulder. "You're Bertha's granddaughter, aren't you?"

I turned to see a short stocky woman with brunette Dorothy Hamill–style hair gazing at me with her eyebrows raised in a question. Horror washed over me. She was the mother of a handsome football player who lived on the same street as my granny—a boy I had a slight crush on but never had the nerve to say anything to.

"I am," I conceded and tried to look her in the eye. My eyes wanted to look anywhere except at her.

She smiled gently. "Well, honey, we can give you a ride if you're willing to wait until after we eat."

"Ah, sure." I looked down at my feet.

She gasped. "Are you okay, honey? You're bleeding. I'm sure they have a first aid kit." Another one of those normal moms, apparently.

A long line of blood ran down my knee sock. Suddenly, my leg started throbbing. "I'm fine," I replied. "I'll be outside waiting. Thank you."

As I pushed the glass door open and walked out, my steps were heavy with embarrassment. I sat down on the curb and stared out across the parking lot into the black sky. Why was this happening to me? Why couldn't I be like the girl in the car with her mom, or like the football player with his mom? Every moment of my life was like drowning in despair.

I tried to stop my hands from shaking as I sat there thinking about the night's events. But I had to keep going if I was to survive. There was no time for a breakdown. The stream of life kept me moving through each situation that should have killed me.

Then I wondered if my dad had made it home. Part of me hoped he had ended up killing himself. At that thought, my conscience rode me hard at what an awful daughter I was. I was supposed to be loyal to him, right? In the heart of Kentucky, family was everything. Blood was the most important tie you could have to someone, and in that moment, I wished I could bleed myself dry.

Moving from elementary school to junior high can be strange and unsettling. Add to it living in a large house with a man who got high most every evening and barely noticed I was there, and well, it made my gut twist. Even so, I found ways to occupy myself. In the summer before my seventh-grade year, I still played with my Barbies and found ways to create my own friends, sort of.

A small ridge of plants sat up the hill from our house, and I would sit outside in that short grouping and pretend they were people and we were a city. I made myself the mayor and would tell them all my secrets. I made a world where they loved me and thought everything I did was brilliant. Hours were spent playing in the dirt there and talking to the plants because there was no one else around. The one girl who lived near me wore cute outfits, curled her hair, and even wore makeup. She thought I was stupid for playing with my dolls and sitting among the plants, so she wouldn't hang out with me.

The summer blurred into dirt, heat, and loneliness.

I was relieved when my dad told me we were moving to my granny's. I didn't know it at the time, but our house had been repossessed by the bank and we were evicted. His seemingly perfect little white house was gone. My dad had it built to save his marriage to Kay, yet it had turned into hell on earth. It was as if I could breathe again, leaving that place where my clothes were in boxes and I slept on a mattress in the corner of my empty room.

My granny was all soft wrinkled skin and tea rose perfume. She represented unconditional love, and I absolutely loved being with her. She enrolled me in the local middle school and even signed me up for basketball. It felt like a dream, and life seemed almost normal. Normal!

My dad relinquished some of his parenting of me to his mother, although "parenting" for him meant keeping me as his possession whenever someone wanted to take me away, like my birth mom. He never showed real concern for me. Most times he actually seemed to hate me for existing. I could never understand why I had been born, because I always seemed unwanted.

I felt like I could relax a bit at my granny's. I slept on the cot at the end of her bed and my dad took the spare room.

Seventh grade started, and I was glad that I knew some of the kids since I had gone to grade school with them. That relief was short-lived, however, because I didn't know how to fix my hair or anything about makeup. I was more tomboy than girly-girl. Gazing at other girls who had hot-rolled hair and perfect makeup had me admiring them with a sort of awe. How did they know how to do all of that? It was a grim reminder of my gaping hole of no mother.

I would go home and stare at my thin face in the mirror and try to figure out how to put on makeup or make my mostly boy clothes look a little more girly. My status as a tomboy wasn't made any less apparent by my participating in basketball, but I found a certain amount of solace in playing. Basketball gave me a lose sort of family. We would practice and play as a unit. And because I had a little bit of height, I was the center. I began to lose myself in the game.

Things fell into a beautiful rhythm for me. School, basketball practice, and coming home to my granny's kind face waiting at the door, ready to serve me a hot meal and a Pepsi-Cola, topped with watching her guilty pleasure, *Guiding Light*. This was probably one of the best times of my life. My dad began to blend into the background like a distant hum since he didn't drink at my granny's.

It was during this safety that a weird sort of dichotomy appeared. The inklings of ending my life sitting on the steps of the Wendy's restaurant that night began to take deeper root. It defied logic that I even thought about it, but sitting on the walk of my granny's house and experiencing a rejection from a would-be boyfriend, I thought seriously about dying. I had no idea how I would do it, but it was a seductive solution to the terror and confusion that was my dad. The lure of peace was almost an overwhelming thought.

Sitting on the bendy prickliness of the artificial grass of the walkway of granny's house, I lifted my wrist to gaze at the faint blue lines underneath my creamy skin. With a pop bottle lid, I dug into the flesh of my wrist. It wasn't deep, but another feeling accompanied the pain—a feeling of release. In my desire to kill myself, I also found a desire to cut.

Conversely, God began to seek me out in small, gentle ways. My granny loved God and would unashamedly talk about him with us, despite what my dad thought about non-Catholics. He was a devout Catholic and held tightly to the notion that no other faith could go to heaven. Everyone else was doomed to hell in his eyes, and he never missed a chance to share that with a person. However, when it came to his own mother, he could never say he thought she would go to hell, even though she was a Protestant. *Every* other Protestant deserved hell, just not her.

I loved the Catholic church for the security it brought me. I was surrounded in ceremony and knew what to expect, and it made me curious about who God was. But I didn't understand God as loving and concerned with me until my granny explained it. I wasn't ready to accept all he was, but it planted small seeds in my head.

As I rushed down the sidewalk in my basketball uniform, a certain excitement thrummed through me. The coach had picked me to be the starting center, and I could hardly keep a sane thought in my head. Each step brought me closer to the middle school, which sat roughly a half mile away.

I tried not to think too much about the fact that no one was coming to cheer me on. While I could understand my granny not coming because she had no vehicle and wasn't able to walk the half mile, I couldn't reconcile my dad's not coming. Instead, he constantly called me stupid and told me I'd never amount to anything—or said the thing that always felt the worst of them all, that somehow I was just like my birth mother.

I shook my head and tried not to think about all of it. I was going to start, and as the center no less. I didn't want to let Coach Adkins down.

As I approached the gym, some of my teammates were arriving with their parents. My gut twisted at the sight of them, but I pushed the bad thoughts down. This was not going to ruin my night.

We walked up the rough stone steps and entered the gym. The faint smell of dust and industrial cleaner hit me in the face. My footsteps squeaked on the floor as I glanced up to the squawking fan at the top of the far wall trying to pull in cool air. The building was old, and while it did offer some heat in the winter, in the summer the lack of air conditioning made the room a sweat box.

After most everyone arrived, we sat on our bench waiting for the game to begin while Coach Adkins went over the plays we had practiced. Before long, the ref blew the whistle and I stood up.

Coach Adkins gave me a pat on the back, and I approached the center of the court. The other team's center was lanky and slightly taller than me. She pressed her lips tight when she glared at me, bending her knees preparing to jump. I took the same stance and stern game face.

Up went the ball. She was able to tap it first and the game began.

Throughout the night I heard cheers of other players' names from parents in the stands. At times, I'd see family and friends standing and clapping. Sometimes people would clap for me if I had the ball, but mostly it was like each player had their own little cheering station— except me. I gritted my teeth.

We ended up winning the game. All the other players were celebrated by their parents, but not me. I stood there staring as everyone left to go out to eat or home with parents, all to celebrate. I could barely lift my feet as I started the walk home in the fading light of day. Brilliant crimson tore across the fading blue of the sky as the sun began its descent. Despite all its glory, I couldn't even begin to appreciate it. I was alone.

Hanging my head, I whispered, "Way to go, Jenny. Great game."

During my middle school years, I developed an odd sort of disassociation with my identity. I began to pretend I was someone else named Garrett Lee. All of my notes to my friends were signed with that moniker. The name gave me such a pleasant sensation, and I was able to make her into whatever I wanted. She didn't have the ugly, dark past or the horrible outlook on the future. Now I realize that Garrett Lee was who I wished I could have been at the moment when I felt most destroyed. I didn't want to be Jenny Butler any longer. I wanted to be Garrett Lee.

Garrett Lee was in control, confident, and artistic. She could command a room and make friends with everyone. She was tough and straightforward and not afraid of anyone. If anything, people should be afraid of her. The pretending was blurry to a degree but really empowering. If I retreated to her identity, then I was safe.

I even asked my friends to call me Garrett Lee. I now see that this mirrored what I had started in second grade—the storytelling. My stories were beautiful worlds that I could retreat to. My mind reveled in the freedom that Garrett Lee brought me.

Becoming a young woman during that time seemed so confusing. It's probably like this for most girls dealing with hormones and how they change the body, but I didn't have much help in understanding it. My granny did things like buy me my first bra, but didn't really talk to me about girl things or what was happening to me.

I felt androgynous. So that was how I lived—sort of half girl, half boy. I was a girl when I went to church with my granny, and when I was me the rest of the time, I shifted to the boy or tough-girl persona.

While I couldn't permanently change my name to Garrett when I was in middle school, I did make a shift in my real name at fifteen. This was another moment of disassociation. I no longer wanted to be Jenny with a y, but I wanted to be Jenni with an i, which to me was short for Jennifer. My father ridiculed me telling me that I was just like my birth mother, who was born with one name but legally changed it when she was eighteen.

Still, I settled into the change and ignored his words. After all, my dad called me stupid or idiot most of the time anyway, so what did it matter if I changed one letter in my name?

It was another weird way to survive, becoming something or someone else. Even now, I get questions about my name, about what do I prefer to be called, whether it is Jen, Jenni, or Jennifer. I never allow anyone to call me Jenni beyond my family. "Jenni" is someone I never want to be again.

CHAPTER 12

breaking the dam

"And you kind of know the rest of the story," I told my counselor, again rubbing at my palm with my thumb.

"I don't know how you ended up living here in this area."

I chuckled. "That's a funny story. Emma and I got into a fight over doing the dishes."

The counselor shifted as the corners of her lips lifted. "How is that funny?"

"Well, it wasn't funny at the time, but looking back it's funny. And as hard as that moment was, I now know God used it to get me out of Collins and into this area."

"Tell me about it. What happened?"

Chuckling, I squared my shoulders and let out a slow breath. "Emma and her husband really tried to be like parents to me, even as young as they were. She wanted me to do the dinner dishes and I refused. When her husband demanded I do them, a huge argument broke out between them and they didn't talk all night. He actually slept on the couch. In the morning she agreed with him that I should do them.

"Knowing that she didn't want Rosa to have custody of me, I threatened to call Rosa and say I wanted to live with her. I figured

Emma would stop me. She didn't, no matter how far I took the threat. Eventually I did end up calling Rosa, and the next day she showed up at Emma's and off I went."

"What were you thinking in that moment?"

I picked a stray piece of lint from my pant leg, then stood up and folded a leg underneath me as I sat. "I thought she would stop me, that she would cave to my objections to the dishes. But she didn't. She let me go. When I was getting into the car, she handed me a letter that I still have today. She was just too young to try to be a parent to a seventeen-year-old. Who could blame her? I was pretty difficult. I'm not sure why. I was pretty reckless in how I lived back then."

The counselor brushed her dark hair off of her shoulders. "You don't know why?" She appraised me with her pale-blue eyes.

Yeah, I knew why. Of course I did. "I, uh, didn't feel worthy to live. I wished every day I was dead." I didn't look up. I couldn't. A weight settled on my chest, and I almost couldn't breathe. Wiping my hands on my legs, I sucked in a breath through my mouth.

"Do you still feel that way? Not worthy to be alive?"

My legs itched to flee as my heart took off pounding. I waved my hand. "Pfft." When I looked at her, she raised her eyebrows and waited. *Okay, okay, okay. What do I say?* "Yeah," I admitted.

"Why would you think you aren't worthy to be alive?"

Okay, here we go. Why not just tell her what I really am? I took a sip of my soft drink. Putting on the ridged lid, I twisted it and placed the bottle at my feet with the label facing out. "Because of what happened. My dad didn't love me. He hurt a lot of girls. My mother didn't love me. I feel dirty."

"But those are just things that happened. They weren't you and they're not who you are."

I twisted in my seat. I really needed to set her straight. "You know, even a police officer who arrested my dad blamed me. I'm sure more people do. He said I should have known better."

That was true. I should have known better. I should have *been* better. But something essential in me was broken in a way I couldn't fix. "I should have done something!" The explosion of words surprised me.

"What could you have done? I mean, did you actually know what to do?"

"No." I hadn't known at the time how to get help for the girls or myself. How could I? Every day was living in survival mode. No one ever talked about calling social workers or getting help for abuse.

"Then how can you say you're guilty of anything?"

"Because! I should have...I should have done something! Anything! But I didn't. I just let those girls be abused."

"But did you? You didn't know how to get help. Your father was the only person you had in your life. You had no power over what he did or where you could go. So, what are you guilty of?"

Tears began to stream down my face. "Of being born." The admission surprised me, even though it was a self-proclaimed truth. If I was guilty of anything, it was that. I should have never been born. My parents should have never had the ability to have me, and God should have killed me as an infant.

"Why do you think that?"

I shifted in my chair and resisted the urge to scream. "Because," I stammered, "I know me and I know what I've done. Who I am, even."

"But you were powerless in the situation. And you aren't guilty of what your father did."

I nodded like I had accepted that, but I really hadn't. The smear on my soul couldn't be washed away with the simple asking of a question.

You don't know me. You have no idea who I really am. How can I listen to you when you don't get who I am?

I got through the rest of the session but quit listening at some point because I couldn't get past my own shame. But her question kept sneaking up on me, invading my thoughts, pressing in. I began to pray over it and ask God what this was all about.

Just like my counselor's question, God began to creep up on me.

The sun streamed in through the counselor's window, creating slanted squares on the carpet. I scanned the room, stopping on awards and books on the nearby shelf. The peace of the room surrounded me with comfort.

Before my counselor could start, I offered, "You know, I tried counseling before. I didn't get to see him long, but I did try."

She smiled. "Oh yeah? What happened?"

I shrugged. "He moved to a different city. I only saw him three times. He was a lay counselor with a church."

"Want to share anything about it?"

"If you want to hear it."

"Sure."

The year I lived with my mother during my final year of high school was one of the hardest of my life. We were two people thrust together to act as if we were mother and daughter, when in reality we were two strangers joined by blood. Not a great situation.

I made it to graduation and entered college, which was about the time my dad was released from prison. During my freshman year, he wrote me a letter asking to see me after his release, and added some not-so-nice comments about Rosa. She got a hold of the letter and made me chose—either live with her and not see him, or see him and live elsewhere. When I couldn't immediately choose, she showed me the door.

Fortunately, a friend of mine introduced me to a family who had a spare room and a lot of love to give. I lived with them for a year as I tried to get my bearings, then eventually married a wonderful man I had gone on a first date with a few days before Rosa threw me out of her house.

Once we were married, I discovered intimacy was almost impossible at first. I would get violently sick and would sob at any attempt. I didn't understand my own reaction to something that should have been beautiful and wonderful. Instead, I felt like I hated my own body and anything related to sex.

I prayed, asking God to help me understand what was happening. None of it made sense. I thought the magic of being married would somehow transform the act of sex, but it didn't. Not at first, anyway. I had to try to work through some of what I had been taught by my father through both observation and blatant abuse.

In looking for a church home, I soon discovered that those were places riddled with landmines. It seemed I couldn't be completely real about who I was. After all, there were expectations, rules, and ways of showing you were a Christian that I couldn't live up to. I felt my brokenness and flaws with every breath I took, all the while begging God to change me, to make me something else or someone else.

I was crazy needy, craving attention and understanding, but didn't know how to verbalize it. So I kept my secrets inside. The few times I did share how I felt, I was met with warnings about watching what I said because I didn't want to disrespect God with how depressed and angry I really was. While I knew God loved me, he didn't seem safe enough for me to say what I was really feeling. My emotions were unsafe yet again. Another reason to despise who I was.

Things began to change when my husband and I started attending a Vineyard Church in Cincinnati, Ohio. It felt decadent and permissive to wear jeans to church and carry my cup of coffee to my seat. People were all shapes and sizes, with some having atypical haircuts with alternative colors. The church had a magnetic pull I didn't want to resist. We planted our stake firmly in the accepting soil of that place.

As we attended, I made a new friend, Louise. She was young but a recovering alcoholic who was newly married. She was the first believer I met who was self-possessed and confident in her walk with God and his acceptance of her.

Louise began to talk to me about who I was, pushing me to tell my story to her. And as much as I had kept the secrets from most people, there was another part of me that was desperate to be known, for someone to know it all and not be fazed by it—to tell me I was okay and what happened was horrible.

It was in my unsteady stepping out to tell her that led to her introducing me to my first counselor. She pushed me to him after a night where I got incredibly drunk and tried to drown myself in my bathroom tub. It was a weak attempt, but had I thought of other ways to do it in my foggy mind, I would have succeeded. I sat fully dressed, soaked to the bone, my long hair in a wet curtain around my face as I said I didn't want to be alive anymore. The pain was simply too much.

Louise convinced Bill to take me to the hospital to test me for alcohol poisoning and possible commitment to the psych ward. I remember flashes of talking to a doctor and his asking me if I wanted to hurt myself. I lied and said I didn't. They had no choice but to let me go home, telling Bill that he could call and get my blood alcohol results in a few days if he wanted to know. He never called and neither did I.

I found myself with Louise in a support group for people with addictions and emotional issues. She had invited me and I went, although I never thought I had any "issues." I had pain, I had self-hate and a lack of desire to live. Were those "issues"? It didn't seem that way; they were just part of my identity. Although, when faced with the reality of who God was and how he saw me, I felt like I stood on the other side of a great gulf that I couldn't get across no matter what I did. He was on one side—perfect, holy, awesome—and I was clear on the other. An orphan in the house of God.

The group was led by a man named Gerald Ross who was a radio personality on a local Christian station and a lay counselor. Much like a guide, he gave a short introduction on a particular subject and then navigated us through group discussion. It was difficult staring into the faces of other women, hearing their stories and feeling able to share a little of mine. It wasn't the same as a one-on-one discussion with some-one; it was telling it to a group of women who didn't judge. I learned that Gerald also did one-on-one counseling. After hearing a bit of my story, a small bit, he invited me to talk to him.

Most of our talks were surface level, as I didn't want to tell him everything. It seemed I subscribed to the "bomb-lobbing" admission of things and then retreated emotionally. It was a litmus test of sorts. I would admit one thing and watch his reaction. His face would never change no matter what I shared. He offered support and walked me through trying to process my past.

One day I shared some details about what my father had done and my guilt in it.

"You think you are to blame?" Gerald asked, a look of disbelief on his face.

The pillow he kept on his sofa was pulled onto my lap, and I began to take apart the knotted part of the fringe. It was a nervous habit that he didn't seem to mind. In fact, I had been systematically taking it apart little by little. He laughed that it was my pillow.

"Yes," I admitted, looking down at the pillow. "If I hadn't lied at the trial or burned evidence or if I'd thought of what to do when my father was doing the things he was doing, then he would have been stopped." I wouldn't look up. I couldn't. My guilt was heavy, a burden I carried daily. I couldn't push it out of my head or reason with it. It was an insidious friend, or perhaps fiend, who coated my insides black. There was no washing the shame away.

"It wasn't your fault what your dad did. He was a grown man." Gerald's carefully crafted face began to show a crack of anger. Was he mad at me? Was he lying, or did he really believe I wasn't to blame? I couldn't tell. "Listen to me, Jen," he went on indignantly. "Your father was the only one guilty in this. It was his fault for what he did. You were a victim just like the girls. You are not at fault. I certainly don't see you as guilty, and neither does God."

My gaze jerked up as tears slid down my face. "What?" I whispered.

He shifted his weight and leaned back. "God says you are innocent." His tone was matter of fact like he believed it.

Could it be true? Could God see me as innocent?

The sorrow I'd always carried pulled me into its torrent, like a raging river, to drown me. My tears poured out so quickly that I couldn't stop them. All the pain, guilt, and fear were overwhelming me. I slid off the couch onto the floor with my back against the sofa and my head buried in my hands, weeping hysterically.

Gerald got up, sat down on the sofa, and stroked the back of my head, just like the preacher who had told me that God loved me, when I was seventeen. I cried harder, leaning on Gerald's leg and sobbing, mourning, lost in my deep well of emotion.

Gerald didn't say a word, simply let me cry against his leg while he stroked my hair. I couldn't stop. I was bleeding out emotionally. It reminded me of John Hiatt's song "Thirty Years of Tears." Whatever had broken in me was as old as I was and was determined to get out regardless of my tenuous delusion of control.

After a while, Gerald leaned into me and told me to stay as long as I needed. He had another client and had to go. After patting my arm and apologizing, he quietly left the room. His voice was a low murmur outside the door, probably telling someone not to disturb me, because no one from his office did.

Eventually my tears stopped, and I wiped my swollen eyes and tried to catch my breath. A wave of embarrassment hit me, and heat filled my face. Had I really lost it like that?

I jumped up, gathered my things, and rushed out of the office.

CHAPTER 13

value

"Jen, I want to talk about your value and purpose. I hear you talk about that a lot."

I squirmed on the sofa at my counselor's question. Value. Purpose. Admittedly, I did talk about them a lot, especially since I felt like I had neither.

"Let's start with value."

I stared blankly at her. This was a hot button because, try as I might, I couldn't conjure up any feelings of worth. If anything, I struggled with why I was still alive—not with the same intensity that I once did, but I struggled nonetheless. "Okay," I said slowly. This subject matter seemed as insurmountable as always.

"Well, how do you feel about yourself and your value?" she asked.

"That I'm not worth much. That I should've never been born. That everything I've suffered has reduced me to a broken, half person." That was the truth. I'd always felt as if I shouldn't be alive, that my being was a mistake, no matter how much I wanted to think God loved me and wanted me now. Where had he been when the abuse was happening?

I knew there were levels of respectability in the church. Leaders had a higher level than regular attendees. Then there was the lower level of the church, and that was where I fit. Honestly, I applied that thinking to society at large and not just with the church. Therefore, it was a natural jump that I didn't feel worthy in the church either.

I saw it too, played out a million times over in some churches. If someone was broken in any way, they were patronized and talked down to, but never really listened to or loved through the brokenness to wholeness. They were tolerated, not accepted.

"Well, let's suppose for a minute you encounter a little girl who has been through horrendous abuse. She is standing before you. What do you say to her about what she's been through and how she feels?"

I could see that little girl before me, tear trails on her face, matted hair hanging down in dirty cords, her big eyes regarding me. My instinct said to hold her, to pull her into my arms and comfort her. "I would tell her how sorry I am, that it wasn't her fault and that it wasn't fair." My arms ached to hold this imaginary girl, to console the grief that must be eating her alive. I wanted to create a space for her to feel her innocence again.

"Do you think she is guilty? Or shameful?" my counselor pressed.

"No!" I almost shouted. To think that it was at all her fault was perverse. She was a little girl. "How could any of it be her fault? She couldn't change what was done to her."

"Does she have value?"

"Of course she does." What a dumb question. Who would even ask that?

"Why does she have value?"

That backed me into a corner, and I considered it. She was a human life and, through no fault of her own, a victim of those around her. "Because she is a human, and all life is valuable."

She nodded. "Then what makes you any less valuable than her?"

In my mind, the little girl's face changed to my own as a child. I sucked in a breath at the image. "Well," I said, trying to frame my reply in a way that made sense. "I'm different."

"How are you different?" she asked, leaning forward in her chair.

"Because I know what I've done. I know what I'm guilty of. I'm broken, dirty, and shameful. My value is diminished."

"Would you say that to the little girl? Is her value diminished by what has happened to her?"

"No. She wasn't complicit in what happened to her."

"And you were?"

"Yes, I was."

"How?"

"I didn't tell anyone. I didn't reach out for help." Really, I was thinking I was guilty for simply being born.

"Did you know you could get help?"

"No."

"Then how are you complicit?"

"I...Well, I guess I wasn't. But I feel like I should have known somehow."

"You couldn't just know it. You were a child and a young teenager when this stuff occurred. It wasn't your fault what someone else chose to do. It wasn't your fault your parents did what they did. They are responsible for their actions, not you."

I stared at my hands, my eyes filling with tears. I carried so much guilt for things that happened to me, and it mingled with shame and crippled me emotionally.

Our session ended with her giving me an assignment to research what gives a person value, and that evening, I began to write it out.

What gives a person value? I've been challenged with finding an answer to this. I honestly cannot say.

Is it what a person does? No, I cannot say it is, because severely disabled individuals have value, and some cannot do much beyond love. So, they cannot "do," so that cannot be what determines value.

Is it who they are? Like do they do extraordinary things? Probably not considering most people just do very average things. I still think they have value.

Is it their occupation or their purpose? No, because some people have very meaningless jobs and they still have value, I think.

Is it what they do for others? No, because sometimes people are too old to do for others, and children take more than they give. Still, they have value.

What is it, then? Is it just because we are human? Just that we are alive and we breathe air? Who is the one who determines value? Do we have value because we "feel" like we have value? Is it that subjective? What if someone else "feels" like I don't have value? Does that make my value less?

I am having a hard time with this. I just think the explanation must be so simple, so basic, or something innate in our living.

When I looked at the paper with all I had written, I asked God to reveal it to me. This "knowing" that people had value was like being in a conversation and not being able to recall a word that I knew was somewhere in my brain but I couldn't find it; I knew it will come to me later, but in that moment its loss was frustrating.

Value felt like bullcrap to me. It might sound sacrilegious, but I didn't believe that just because Jesus died for me, I was valuable as an individual. That told me that he did it for the fate of mankind, right? To reconcile us to God? This was what I was thinking.

Right away, God gave me three Bible passages to ponder:

Though my father and mother forsake me, the Lord will receive me (Psalm 27:10 NIV).

"For I know the plans I have for you," declares the LORD, "plans to prosper you and not to harm you, plans to give you hope and a future" (Jeremiah 29:11 NIV).

"Can a mother forget the baby at her breast and have no compassion on the child she has borne? Though she may forget, I will not forget you! See, I have engraved you on the palms of my hands; your walls are ever before me" (Isaiah 49:15–16 NIV).

I stared at the last passage. The words *Though she may forget, I will not forget you!* stood out to me. The verse admitted the possibility that our parents would forget us, or not nurture us, but promised that God would always be there for us. Psalm 27:10 hit the same nerve. It also conceded that our parents would forsake or deny us, but that God would receive us, or raise us.

This was the beginning of my first acknowledgment of my value to God. When I read the first chapter of Ephesians, that addressed how we are chosen into sonship because of God's love. I began to realize that my value resided in God. Because he made me and spared not even Jesus from me, I did have value. It wasn't because of my occupation or something I could earn. My value was a given and couldn't be taken away because of what was done to me or who my parents were. The verses showed me that rejection could come from parents but that God was there to pick up the pieces. I simply needed to let him.

I continued to work hard on determining who I was and letting the truths of who God said I was penetrate my soul. I'm not going to lie; it was a profoundly deep struggle. It took a few years of working on that and continuing to work through everything in counseling before I could see cracks of light getting through the hard shell of darkness around me.

CHAPTER 14

becoming me

About a year after I started counseling, I began to dabble in acting. My creative side screamed to get out and to try things I had always wanted to do. So I signed up for acting classes, pursued representation from an agent, and began the harried process of auditions and rejections.

During this time, I was introduced to a man with striking blue eyes and a smoothly shaved head who would become my acting coach. He had an easy smile and a nonjudgmental demeanor that made it easy to try, fail, learn, and try again.

While sitting in his living room one afternoon, he leaned back in a plush chair, gazing at me with his hands casually resting in his lap. "So, Jen, tell me your story."

Blinking a few times, I shifted my weight on the couch, "What do you mean, my story?"

After a sip of his water, he said, "You know, your story. Like where you come from, what makes you, you."

I looked away as heat rushed to my face. "I don't really have a story."

"Sure you do. We all do. I want to hear yours. You've said things here and there, little inklings of something more that has happened in your life, and I'm curious. As actors, we use those experiences from our lives to be able to connect with any character we play." He waited with such an expectant confidence.

I wasn't sure I wanted to jump into all the details of my life, but we had built a certain level of relational currency, so I considered it to my own chagrin. "Well, my story is completely messy. It would take a while to tell it all to you." I hoped that with my warning of how long it would take, he'd give up.

"I've got all day," he said easily. "Start from the beginning." He shifted in his seat to get more comfortable and waited for me to begin.

The words were hard to get out at first. My story was ugly from the very beginning of my life, not the idyllic childhood with loving parents, birthday parties, and family celebrations. It was terror, mental illness, extreme loneliness, helplessness, and sexual abuse. In that moment I wanted to be anyone other than who I was.

Amid multiple glasses of water, several tissues, and lots of deep breaths, I found myself telling a man I deeply respected the gritty details of my life. For whatever reason, I told him almost everything. After three hours, I got to the end and waited in fear for the rejection I was sure was coming. With nothing more to say, I stared at my feet in shame.

I heard the rustling of his clothes as he rose from his seat. To go throw up? To go contemplate how to ask me to leave? My mind raced with the possibility of his response. Suddenly his feet appeared in my line of vision. When I glanced up at him, he stood with his arms open and a look of compassion on his face.

I rose and embraced him. The warmth of him holding me was like a balm to my soul.

"That was very brave of you, Jen," he breathed against my hair. "Well done."

Awkwardly, I pulled away, unable to make eye contact with him. In telling him my story, I believed I had shifted from young actress and writer to broken, ruined Jenni.

He must have sensed my unease, because he said, "Look at me, Jen."

I obeyed and met his kind eyes. "I'm proud of you."

Proud.

It took a few moments for the words to sink in, but I somehow trusted what he said.

A few weeks later in another acting coaching session, he said slowly, "Jen, you know how you told your story to me? Well, I'm starting a new storyteller's show in Cincinnati. Do you know what *The Moth* is?"

I shook my head.

"It's a show where people tell snippets of their true-life stories. Go home and find it on the internet and listen to it. Because I want you to consider participating with some of your own story."

Swallowing hard, I gaped. "In public?"

He gave a small chuckle. "Yep. That's exactly what I mean." Giving me a sideways hug, he reassured, "Go listen to the show, think about it, and let me know."

Later that evening I scoured the web looking for *The Moth*. I listened to many short stories from people talking about abandonment, funny happenings, and gut-wrenching sorrow. And my acting coach thought I was brave? After discussing it with my counselor and Bill, I found the courage to say yes to my coach. I thought that would be the hardest part of it, but the most challenging was yet to come.

My coach introduced me to his co-producer of the show, a stocky man with wavy dark curls and a dark beard. Whatever hair my coach lacked, his partner seemed to have. After the introductions, my coach asked me to relay some of my story to his partner.

I didn't think I would be able to do it. I stared at this burly man who was all but a stranger to me, considering how to start. Summoning every ounce of courage I possessed, I began. This time, however, before I was far along, the producer asked me to talk about one part that related to the subject of their first show—fear.

Fear and I were intimately acquainted, so to tell of how it operated in my life became easier. I could process my story from a subject and not from shame. That little shift in focus made it slightly easier to tell.

After that first night with the producer, I had many more opportunities to tell my story, over and over again, whittled down so I recounted only the parts relevant to the subject.

Then the night of the show arrived. It was held at a theatre in downtown Cincinnati, located in the art district. I ended up being the kickoff speaker to the very first show in that series.

A hundred people crammed into the ground-floor theatre to hear our stories. The harsh spotlights eclipsed any faces that were in the audience, so it was like speaking to the dark. Once I began, the words drifted out of me in an easy flow that came from much practice.

After a couple more speakers, we had a break, and the house lights were brought up. People rushed out to smoke or get drinks from the bar. I opted to get some water from a counter in the back.

As I filled my glass, a throat cleared behind me. "Excuse me," said a hesitant female voice.

Turning, I greeted a woman who was twisting her hands in front of her. Beside her, a pleasant man offered a slight grin. "Your story...wow," she said. "That was so courageous of you."

"Thank you." I gave her a smile as we stood in an awkward pause.

She chewed on her lip, then stammered, "My mother was schizophrenic. I never told anyone, ever. Not until now."

I felt my face relax into compassion. I understood her hesitancy.

"I never let friends come over. I hid it from everyone as much as I could. I couldn't tell anyone about all the crazy things she did at home."

"I'm sorry. That must have been hard. I understand. I really do."

Her face softened in our moment of camaraderie. Then she turned to the man beside her. "Oh, this is my husband."

I shook their hands. "Nice to meet you."

Her and my hands had just released when she blurted, "We decided to never have kids of our own because we don't want to pass on the gene for mental illness."

What do you say to that? A surprised "Oh," escaped my lips at this very personal admission. A profound sense of sadness enveloped me at the price she was willing to pay at the possibility of giving to her offspring what she had seen in her mother. A parent's mental illness was robbing her of something precious, even though it wasn't a surety. I couldn't judge her decision, but I did feel sadness at her loss. Maybe that was her only way to control something that was birthed out of extreme chaos.

After a little more conversation, I watched her go back to her seat and was overwhelmed with the realization that she had just told me what she was unable to tell anyone before now. In my telling, she found the wherewithal to tell her own dark secret.

This was what I needed to do. I needed to tell, to shine the light on the darkness so that others could come into the light instead of scurrying to the shadows.

God was in me telling my story. I just wasn't sure to what end.

When I met Carolyn, I immediately liked her. Her red hair flowed all around her face, and her laugh was wildly infectious. I was introduced to her by someone who thought she could give me some life coaching. I'd never heard of a life coach, but from what I knew of her, she was insightful, and so I wanted to see what God might have for me.

With her legs pulled up on the chair, she leaned back and listened to me with a serene gaze as I told her about my past and my life now. Her patient openness demolished a few of my hesitant barriers that would have kept me from sharing the more intimate details of my life, like "Oh, my father was a sex offender," "I wanted to kill myself for the majority of my life," etc. No, I told her those things readily as I gazed into her eyes. The tenor of her said "no judgment," so I dumped everything in the course of two hours.

When we were ready to end our session, she said something that broke down a wall that I didn't know was there: "I think Dad wants you to sit down with a pad of paper and a pen and write that way. Throw out the software you use to write and get quiet. Dad wants to say something to you. Ask him what he wants you to write." *Dad* was her unconventional reference to God.

Her advice tore at me on two levels. One, I'd spent the last few years learning to use the tools of my craft and had seemed to find a weird rhythm in using them. To throw them out as a way to try to write seemed off. Two, I asked God all the time what to write. So that question had been thrown up to God multiple times. Nothing new there. But while grumbling in my heart, I said, "Okay." Wrestling with that later, I sat down and quieted my heart to listen to God.

I was immediately taken back to when I was a child and I acted out sexually. This was something I rarely shared because of all the shame associated with it. In fact, I'm not even sure I mentioned it to my counselor. Why was God bringing this to mind now?

Straightening, I blinked my eyes to dispel the memories that floated around in my head. Nausea ran over me. Everything in me wanted to forget that I had ever done that. I wanted to run away and hide and pretend none of it had ever happened. After all, only I knew about it, with maybe the exception of a few people who knew me at age seven. Of what benefit would it be to look at it now?

I'm not going to lie. I wanted to run. I wanted to chuck all of those thoughts out the window. But I considered that the life coach had been brought to me for a reason and maybe, just maybe, that even with as uncomfortable as this was, there was purpose in it somewhere. I fought the profound urge to ignore her suggestion.

In my overwhelming disgust and shame for how I responded as a child to the porn, God began to speak to me. And I began to have these seemingly random things come to mind about how victims' bodies respond, in the moments of attack, without any intent on their part. It was complete biology devoid of intent. That was me. I was seven, responded to the abuse, acted out, and it was devoid of intent. But I couldn't shake the confusing feeling that I was complicit in abuse, that my body's response and my acting out were evidence of not being a victim but a participant. That feeling swarmed me like bees, stinging me deep in my soul.

Floating around on the periphery like a ghost waiting for me to recognize it was a memory I couldn't allow to take shape. The memory, or flash, was something I couldn't decipher at the time it occurred, and so I almost gave up trying to get it now. Only by the grace of God was I going to get what all this was.

During these confusing few days, God spoke clearly to me:

"Look at me, child. Peace is my name; safety is my arms. I am your stronghold and absolute truth. You are mine, and you are not alone in this boat. I have the oars, remember? Stop looking at the world and expecting peace or safety. I am your peace. I am your fortress. Look only at me and your hands and reach to me. Shut off the world and the voices that will scream long and hard to look at them and what they offer. I am your only

source of peace and safety. Look only at me. Find your peace and rest. Let go."

A strange sort of response bled out of that. On one level, I felt reassured and carried by the arms of my Father, but on another, I was healing fatigued. I had thought this process was over and yet here I was again, processing it again. Processing loss—again. Then the image of a little girl walked through my head like a person who was familiar and somehow a resident in the deep recesses of my mind.

At the beginning of October, God spoke again:

"Begin. Start from here. A new thing, something you have not perceived. Reach to me and let me show you. You are mine. Blessed is the man who hears my commands and keeps them. I love your attempts at obedience. Trust me, trust me, trust me. Come closer to the throne of grace, to my loving arms, my protective hands. My hands have been a fear for you because of your earthly dad. Reach to me. You can trust me. I can heal it all."

I prayed and told God that I couldn't work this out, even with his assurances. I didn't understand the overwhelming guilt and the undefined memory. So how could I work it out? I felt powerless in it all. It was at that moment that I saw a child inside me. Small, hazel eyes too big for her face, pink lips, thin brown hair. Skinny and frail, she was desperate to be loved. And incredibly lonely.

Then the strangest thing happened. I watched as that little girl jumped into my arms and laid her head on my shoulder. Suddenly I felt like two people and, truthfully, a little crazy. Why could I see a small child in me like that? There was little Jenny. Jenny with a "y."

God spoke to me again:

"All the shame, pain, and embarrassment must go in the light of my love. You were a child, Jenny. A child. Let Jenny into Jenni. Pick her up. Love her, hold her. Let me work through you to love her. She is ruled by confusion. Let her pour out her heart. I want to bring her peace and give her clarity. I want her to feel love and freedom as a little girl. Love her! Love her! I do, without wavering, without question. I approve of her. She, Jenny, is mine!"

It overwhelmed me. But I knew exactly what God meant. When I was a child, I was always called "Jenny" by my family. They spelled my name with a "y." But when I reached about fifteen, right around the time my father was deep in his abuse of young girls, I began to spell my name with an "i" on the end because it was short for Jennifer. At the time I made this change without much thought, but God showed me now that I had broken with who I was when I was younger. I figuratively became two people—Jenny with a "y" who had travailed the abuse, lived through the sexual abuse of girls around her, and suffered herself. Somewhere in me I shifted and became Jenni with an "i."

But Jenny came back—or never left, as it were. She remained in the background of my mind waiting, I think, for me to see her. I didn't know how to look at her and not hate her. How could I hate a child? I couldn't hate someone else, but this was me and I hated that part of me.

An opportunity came for me to go to a local event hosted by our church in which women went to camp overnight on this vast stretch of undeveloped land miles outside of anything urban. I had been to this camp before and had no intention of going back because my prior experiences were mediocre at best. But upon the prodding of a friend, I agreed to go one week before the event.

On the morning of the first day, I sat in worship pondering the words God had been speaking to me about little Jenny. I had a vision of God bringing her before me but not saying a word. I violently pushed her away. She fell into the dirt and God picked her up and brought her back to me. This time I struck her hard and yelled at her at the top of my lungs. She flung back like a rag doll and landed hard. Again, God said nothing and brought her to me, and I violently struck her, pummeling her with all my anger and fury. She never fought back, and God remained silent. But I was enraged.

In the midst of thousands of women worshipping God, I was having visions of attacking that small part of me that was a little girl. Tears came out of me in a torrent, and I wept unrelenting tears. I didn't want to hate that part of me that I could obviously see was a child. But I did. I hated how she acted, the shameful things she did, her body's reaction to the abuse and exposure to pornography. I hated how she began to learn to dwell on sexual things. I wanted nothing to do with her.

Yet here she was, being presented to me by God. In his silence, I knew the difficult thing he was saying. He wanted me to love her. I didn't think I could.

I stumbled back to my campsite, sobbing bitterly and unable to see the dirt beneath my feet through my blurred vision. My site leader appeared, slipped her arm around me, and asked, "You want to talk about it?"

"I can't," I choked out.

She gave an understanding smile but didn't push. "Well, if you want to talk, I'm here."

I nodded but didn't meet her gaze. Shame was weighing me down, knocking me to the lowest place that existed in my identity.

The rest of the day was filled with things that kept me occupied, mostly. Jenny with a "y" waited for me to acknowledge her, but I kept a cold resolution to keep myself together by ignoring her.

At two in the morning, after all the events of day ended, everyone made their way back to the camp. The other ladies were exhausted, so they went to their tents and collapsed. However, two remained—a bubbly, obsessive-includer friend of mine named Taylor and another girl named Jane.

I'm sure it was the Holy Spirit at work in that moment, because the three of us sat under the cover of the tent in the darkness and began to talk. Heat flooded my face, because I knew I was going to tell them what had happened earlier. But in that admission, I would need to divulge a few other things to give them context or it wouldn't make sense.

I began with the vision from earlier in the day—how God had brought me the little me, Jenny, and how I had beaten her in my head. That disturbing vision of how much I hated myself destroyed me, and that was why I had cried so grievously. Then I sucked in a deep breath and admitted something I had only told my husband: I had struggled with an addiction to pornography, although I had broken the cycle successfully a year before. In an odd way, the admission of having been "clean" for a full year seemed to be nullified by the fact that I had viewed porn in the first place. While I loathed porn because it had been used as sexual abuse, I had learned my expressions of sexuality through it and I desired it in an almost uncontrollable way.

Taylor and Jane surrounded me with words of affirmation, understanding, and acceptance. Tears ran down my face, which surprised me since I'd believed that I'd cried them all earlier.

"Why don't you come to the childhood sexual trauma class at church?" Taylor asked. As a childhood survivor of abuse, she led a class that wrapped their figurative arms around survivors and helped them understand who they were and how abuse affects them.

"Okay," I heard myself say.

I let out a heavy sigh. I had told someone—yes, out loud—a shameful secret that I carried. Had that really happened? Yes, it gloriously had.

A few days after I got home, a friend asked, "Hey, did anything happen early on Sunday morning about two a.m.? The Holy Spirit woke me up with a neon sign that said 'Pray for Jen,' so I did. Does that mean anything to you?"

My heart worshipped in that moment. God had surrounded me with the prayers of a friend as I made the admission of something I had tried to keep buried for my entire life. Obviously, God wanted me to begin to talk on this.

The following week, I met with the life coach. I'm not sure where my courage came from, but as I stared at the floor, I admitted all the gory details to her—the porn use, my body's involuntary reaction to it at a young age, and my public masturbation when I was seven years old.

Again, I was met with understanding, compassion, and a gentle word. "I think Dad wants to work on that," she said. "You should listen."

At that point, I began to see that if I really wanted God to be first in this process, I needed to be willing to risk my reputation and expose the truth of where I had been and what I had struggled with. Slowly, I began to fully surrender. God showed me that my addiction to pornography had originated in my childhood, and that the tool of some of my abuse had become a tool for my enslavement as an adult.

Then, Jenny began to speak to me. Her voice made me think she was about four years old. She told me things that she thought, like, "Laps aren't safe." I answered her in my head and decided that however weird it was, I was going to treat her like a separate person in my head.

She told me that she didn't trust Jesus at all because he was a man and men abuse. Actually, the raw language she used was "Jesus has a penis." As irreverent as that may sound, it was a child's response to men in general when men had abuse her. For little Jenny, men were never safe or protective. They may not have always been sexual with her, but she felt no protection from them. So, I got it. She understood that Jesus was a man, and therefore she didn't see him as a protector or safe. That was mind-blowing for me. Little Jenny was *not* sexualizing Jesus; she was expressing a fear of men. She identified him as a man, and couldn't find it in herself to trust him.

During a morning of worship, I had another scene play out in my head. Little Jenny took my hand and looked up at me with her big brown eyes and told me she was sorry for what she had done. She said, "I repent."

I understood what she meant. While she wasn't responsible for any of it, she wanted me to know she was still sorry. I embraced the apology. Then Jesus approached her with a pure white dress with eyelet lace. He knelt before her and presented the dress to her with a smile. She took it, put it on, and began to dance. She danced to the praise music, and it was the most beautiful moment. I began to forgive her, and a crack was formed in my hard heart toward her.

The irony of the eyelet lace dress given to little Jenny in that vision, compared to the eyelet lace gown I was going to die in so many years before, is not lost on me. Jesus was exchanging death for life. All I can do is breakdown in worship over this detail now.

A few weeks later, I walked into my first ever childhood sexual trauma class. The classes had been started to help address the fallout from sexual abuse. It was largely passive for the attendees, as they listened to experts educate on how trauma affects the victim in a variety of ways. I drank it in.

During my second class, an expert began to speak about how one of her clients "spoke" to her inner child and even considered ways in which she could comfort her. She explained that when you experience a trauma, your emotional growth halts in those places. As a result, her client largely treated her inner child as a separate person. I rocked back on my heels. That was how I was treating mine, and this was a thing?

My hand slowly rose.

"Yes?" she said with an expectant grin, her eyes twinkling behind her glasses.

"Um, is that normal? To talk to your inner child, that is?"

"Completely normal." She waved her hand and gave a wide, reassuring smile.

"Wow. Because I do that all the time. We actually have conversations," I breathed in disbelief and gazed around to see the expressions of everyone else. No one gave a harsh glance or any derision at all. Relief flooded me.

"It's really okay," she said.

I nodded and inwardly told little Jenny we were going to continue this journey together. I'm not certain, but I think she giggled in agreement.

Honestly, I put talking to my inner child in the category of being mentally ill. Sybil, anyone? But what I was experiencing wasn't blacking out or having a "personality" take over my body. No, it was a frightened, overwhelmed little girl looking for affirmation. I had an expert in her field looking at me and telling me in no uncertain terms that it was normal. Well, at least I was normal in one way.

Empowered with this information, I allowed myself to actually talk to Jenny. I found her to be innocent and strangled with fear of men, and so to begin to think about Jesus and, to some degree, God, as a safe space blew her mind. It began with little things, like telling her it was okay to hold his hand, that he wasn't going to hurt her. I also explained that sexual organs were just parts of the body that had intentions for life in adulthood. What had happened to her tainted everything.

As I talked to her, Jesus appeared there. He talked to her, looking her in the eye as he brought himself down to her level. Kindness and compassion rolled off of him as he smiled at her. I still can't forget his loving expression when he gave her the white dress that she danced in, the one that, surprisingly, she was still wearing.

Once, though, she turned away from Jesus out of fear. She didn't want to sit in his lap; laps were fearful places for her. So she sat in a chair and turned away from him. Jesus wasn't put off by it. In fact, he simply smiled and let her sit that way, no judgment.

Today, Jenny and I are still on the healing journey, and I don't know how God will move and heal us, but I'm certain Jesus is right there with her and me, leading us, and will one day take us to a new place of healing. Jesus has even shown me that Garrett Lee needs to be brought into wholeness too. That's something I'm working on.

CHAPTER 15

goodbye to dad

For years, I kept my distance from my father. He roamed around Collins, Florida and, on occasion, Ohio. While I didn't have contact with him, my family in Collins felt obligated to keep me up to date. The only time I did keep track of him, although indirectly, was when he was out of work. Then I funneled money through a relative to make sure he had food to eat.

Eventually, my father's mental status declined so much that the State of Kentucky was given involuntary guardianship of him. After that, his overall health seemed to get worse. Then he had a stroke—a massive one that left him with little brain function and in a permanent vegetative state. When I received the call about the stroke, I simply accepted it and felt no need to go see him. After all, I had forgiven him and "declared" that to everyone. So there was absolutely no need for me to see him. I had nothing to say to him or anyone else on the matter.

Then the phone calls and texts started coming from family members, demanding I go and see him. Fifteen days later, I was weary from all the stress I couldn't carry. I didn't want to see him—did I? Did it make me a bad person that I didn't want to go? Couldn't I have said all I wanted to say and have meant it?

Though my breathing hitched, all my tears had stopped by the time

I sat on my well-worn couch, gazing at the once-comforting minty-green walls of my living room. The whirl of thoughts blended into a disjointed hum as I turned everything over and over again in a desperate attempt to make sense of it all.

God, please show me what to do. I don't know what to do!

At any minute, Bill would walk through the door, and with him, his comforting arms that I couldn't wait to have around me. The minutes in waiting stretched out into what seemed like hours. Confusion gripped my brain in a choke hold. Plus, I realized I couldn't remember my drive home from my job ten miles away. Thank you, Lord, that I didn't end up in a wreck.

Laying my head back, I closed my eyes as a wave of embarrassment washed over me at how thoroughly I had lost it at work. Thankfully, my boss knew a few details of the epic battle my family was engaged in over my dad, so he sent me home with little fuss.

The processing of my dad dying and the pressure from my family to see him had drudged up memories that pooled around my feet like a septic tank failure polluting a yard. The sickening recollections, along with harsh words, oozed all over my insides, coating them with a thick sheen of the foulest sludge. It culminated with the incredible breakdown that surprised even me. For all my confidence in my own abilities to cope, the reality made me feel like I would never be free of this—of him.

I let out a heavy sigh and opened my eyes to stare up at the ceiling, hoping God would give me some guidance in what to do. I didn't want to see my father. There seemed to be no reason. I had already forgiven him and said my goodbyes. Nothing more needed to be said or done. So why the nervous breakdown?

A small, accusing voice screamed at me for my inability to normally process my dad's dying. I agreed with the voice. I truly was messed up beyond repair.

Please God. Show me what to do. Help me.

Something touched my arm, and my head jerked up.

Bill sat down and wrapped his arm around me. "Sorry. Didn't you hear me come in?" he asked with concern, his eyebrows pushed down tight over his pale green eyes. His thumb brushed lightly over the top of my hand.

"No." I really was losing my mind. Maybe I was like my dad after all. A fresh wave of hysteria threatened. Many years before, I'd conquered my fear that I was mentally ill like him, so I determined to not lose ground and question my sanity. I was not like my dad. I wasn't.

But really, I didn't know what I should and shouldn't be feeling. There wasn't a manual on how to navigate the murky, troubled waters of my broken family. None of us knew how to process any type of family trauma in a healthy way. Those reactions were akin to someone shooting a bullet at your head and narrowly missing. "Normal" never defined my family, so I shouldn't have expected it in this latest disaster.

Bill let out a heavy sigh and leaned back against the couch, still keeping his strong hand entwined with mine. "What happened today?"

The accusing voice started screaming inside me again.

You are shameful for not seeing your dad.

You probably do want your dad to die.

You haven't forgiven him for all the things he did..

You are a horrible person.

"I, uh, I started crying and couldn't stop. I sat at my desk for as long as I could to get a hold of myself, but I just couldn't pull myself together. So they sent me home."

Bill pulled me closer, and I leaned on his shoulder, welcoming his warmth against me. His fingertips trailed up and down my arm. "Did you get another phone call or email from your family?" he asked gently, almost as if he were talking to a small child.

I could hear his heart beating through the thin shirt that smelled of machinery coolant. Normally, I didn't like to touch his work clothes, but today I didn't care. I needed his touch more. He was here and that was all that mattered. "No. I'm not sure why I'm so upset."

He made a low noise in his throat. "I know why. This whole situation is completely messed up."

"It is," I agreed and blinked back another round of tears that threatened to come. The quiet of the room created a safe place for me to crumble in my husband's arms. "Bill?"

"Hmmm?" His voice vibrated against my ear.

"Do you think I'll regret not going to see him?" My voice was barely a whisper. When speaking to my family, our discussions stabbed out in tense, harsh words because I wouldn't go to my father's bedside and act like the grieving daughter—no matter how they'd tried to guilt me into it. Up to this point, I'd confidently thought I'd have no regrets about it because nothing needed to be said. I'd forgiven him and that was that. What more was there?

Bill sat up a little straighter, the couch creaking slightly under his weight. He cleared his throat. "Well, I don't know. Maybe years from now you might. I really don't know." He pressed a kiss to my head. "What are you thinking?"

Okay, God. If 'I don't know' is your way of telling me to go, I'll go.

My breathing began to get shuddery again. "Well...I...I think...if there is a chance...even a small one, I should go see him."

Bill made a small noise of surprise, and the smell of chemicals from his shirt filled my nose.

I sat up away from him, looking into his eyes. "He may not even know I'm there, and what would it matter anyway?" I said in an attempt to argue with him—or maybe myself. My resolve was wavering.

Bill shrugged. "He might not."

I rested my head back against his shoulder. Then some questions began to bounce around in my head: What if his spirit could hear me? Can spirits hear like the body and soul do? Is the spirit the one place that mental illness wouldn't have ravaged him? The strange consideration began to grow in my head—if a spirit could be rational and could hear me, then it seemed clear that I had to go. What if deep in him, a part of my father was sane? Would he care that I had come? Would I matter to him? Would my words mean anything to him?

I gazed across the living room to my guitars sitting idly in their stands. Like a shooting star in my head, an idea took form, clearing up the haze of uncertainty. "Let's go to Louisville. But I'm not telling my family that I'm going, okay?"

When I sat up to look at Bill again, he gave a small grin. "Okay. Let me go get ready." He got up and headed for the shower.

As the sound of the water echoed, I rose and went to my music book lying on the stand. If my dad had even the faintest chance of hearing me, really hearing me with a part of him unfettered by mental illness, I wanted to do the one thing he had never heard me do—sing. And not only sing, but offer praises to the Father who had created us both.

The intoxicating thought that my dad would hear me with sanity grew within me. It drove me with renewed possibilities despite my fragile state.

The sheets of music scratched together as I started the process of picking songs. What would I want to sing for my dad for the last time I might ever see him? Three songs seemed to leap off the sheets at me, one of which I wrote as a worship leader for a small church a few years prior. I grabbed them and crammed them into my guitar case.

I stood waiting by the door when Bill walked into the kitchen.

His eyes flickered to the guitar and back up to my face. "Why are you taking that?" His fingers brushed through his wavy hair in a questioning gesture.

"I want to sing praises to my heavenly Father with my earthly dad. I don't care that I'll be in an ICU unit."

Bill's lips quirked into a slight smile. "Sounds like a good plan."

Pleasure laced with approval spread across his face, and that confirmed that I was doing the right thing, although I wasn't sure how to pull it off in a hospital. The staff might throw me out, or even have me as a "restricted" visitor. Who knew at this point? It seemed like a Hail Mary.

The drive to Louisville took about two hours from Cincinnati, which allowed me time to prepare. Bill kept a hold of my hand, occasionally giving it a slight squeeze. But we said very little, and my thoughts were a storm in my head as the landscape passed by.

We pulled up to a squat building no more than five stories high that occupied about a half a city block. Its facade was a dull-colored stone that had probably started out as white, and the tiny parking lot told me they didn't have large amounts of visitors. What kind of place was this?

I let out a sigh as I pulled my guitar case out of the back of the car, only to find Bill taking it from my hand.

The cold January air shot through me like daggers. Shuddering, I wrapped my coat tight around me, then paused, contemplating the next few moments. Would it be a fight? Would I be able to see him? Whatever would I say to him? I didn't even know. I'd had millions of comments for him in my head over the years, so many unspoken words, so many aching needs as his daughter. Now, my mind seemed blank as I contemplated the last words I'd ever say to him.

We made our way up to my dad's room, passing people. Some walked by brushing away tears, while others were engaged in normal conversations. But for me, "normal" had no measure in this moment. Thankfully, the blankness soothed me even though an accusing voice said I should be feeling something, anything.

Dad's room was a small square with the hallway side concealed by a curtain. The interior walls were a pleasant beige certainly meant to soothe a troubled soul, but there seemed to be a certain amount of shadow and darkness regardless. The singular window on the exterior wall let in the muted winter light but did nothing to brighten the room.

My dad lay in a huddled mass beneath a white sheet. A blue tube ran to his mouth while the top part of his face was covered with a washcloth. The beeping of his heart monitor competed with the whishing of the breathing machine pushing air into his lungs. I frowned as I heard what sounded like a fair amount of mucus in his throat each time he took in air. It had me wanting to clear my throat.

As I stood taking it all in, a young nurse with dark hair moved past me. "Hello," she said with a pleasant smile, then leaned over a machine to check it.

"Why does he sound like that?" I asked. Right away, I realized I probably should have greeted her first.

She straightened. "He just needs to be suctioned out. The breathing tube gets like that sometimes."

Blinking, I kept my eyes trained on her, silently relaying my displeasure at why it hadn't been done yet. I couldn't figure out my boundaries here. What could I demand? On paper I was his daughter, but in reality, I functioned as more of a stranger. The sense of family entitlement simply wasn't there. Just another moment of trying to figure out "normal" as I went, just like always.

Truth be known, I had run from the very acknowledgment of him, a convicted sex offender and an unmedicated paranoid schizophrenic who for years wreaked havoc on his family and everyone around him. I ran from him and his turmoil years ago. Now here I stood acting like things were fine.

What was I doing here anyway? Maybe this had been a mistake.

She put her hands on her hips and asked gently, "And who are you?"

I bit my lip, eventually finding my voice. "I'm his daughter, Jenni." The words sounded odd as they passed over my lips. To claim a connection between us was ancient, like a fossil frozen in stone.

She grinned again. "I'm Rita, his nurse. Give me a minute and I'll suction him out." A breeze hit my face as she rushed past me.

I stepped farther into the room and stared at my dad. The man I had feared, hated, and loved—not necessarily in that order and often at the same time—lay motionless. He appeared so much smaller. The bigger-than-life man I remembered seemed nothing like the small prone body on a hospital bed.

Holy Spirit, help me through this, I prayed.

I almost gagged when Rita suctioned his throat. When she seemed to be ready to walk out of the room, I asked about why his eyes were covered.

"That's to keep them from drying out. They won't close." She lifted the washcloth to show me.

My breathing hitched as I peered at what were once brown eyes, now a sickly blue color. The skin around them drooped, and his gaze was fixed, as were his pupils.

"The cloth helps keep them moist," she offered as she replaced it. Offering a smile that didn't reach her eyes, she asked, "Do you need anything else?"

"No, thank you," I whispered.

She nodded and all but ran out of the room.

I dragged a chair to the end of the bed and pulled out my sheets of music. After getting out my guitar, I tuned it and looked toward the head of the bed almost as if my dad would suddenly sit up. Then I glanced over to Bill, and he gave me a reassuring nod.

Letting out a strong huff, I glanced to my father. "Dad, I hope you can hear me."

Two lines into "How He Loves Us" by John Mark McMillan, my

voice began to falter from my throat closing with tears. My words quavered, but I kept going. Along with my strained voice, my guitar began to lose tune from the incredibly cold room, but I finished, all the while my playing competed with the echoes of people walking by, intercoms paging doctors, and the machines that kept an opposing rhythm.

Tears streamed down my face, landing with soft thuds on the top of my guitar, but I forced myself to keep going even though my voice barely hit all the notes. The atmosphere was thick with an unseen presence silently watching the collision of the earthly and the heavenly. What could I do but play along?

Gasping for air to steady my hiccupped breathing, I tuned my guitar again and pushed onto "10,000 Reasons" by Matt Redman and Jonas Myrin. I struggled, but as I continued, I focused on God and thanked him as my true Father instead of the man dying before me. Singing the songs became a declaration of sorts, cutting the cord between this man and me with a certain amount of finality. The songs were my stake in the ground in rejecting the lies I had believed my entire life and the false blame I carried over the crimes he had committed.

I realized another unshakeable truth—that this man dying was also fiercely loved by God, regardless of what he had done to me and so many others. What could my dad have been like had he not been plagued with mental illness? The sorrow in that question threatened to suffocate me. I already grieved the loss of never having a normal father, but not once had I ever tried to imagine him as a loving, normal man—offering me comfort and guidance, giving me a pure hug of affection, or telling me he loved me. I needed to push it out of my head if I was going to survive this moment.

I took in a breath and paused. My final song was one that I had written. I stared down at the sheet and felt an odd sense of pleasure bloom at being able to sing this to my heavenly Father while my earthly one could hear.

When that song ended, I set down my guitar, gave a self-deprecating laugh, and whispered, "Sorry I butchered that, Dad. It's been a while since I played them." I stood and walked to my dad's side, then took his ice-cold hand and gazed at it as if for the first time. How odd that it appeared so much smaller than I remembered. How long had it been since I last held his hand? When I was four, maybe. I pressed my hand against his and realized our hands were about the same size. I can't explain why, but those moments shifted my dad from a giant to a person. I carefully laid his hand back down and covered it with the sheet.

Reflexively, I leaned down and kissed the top of his head despite the smell of urine and stale sweat. Then I whispered into his ear the words I thought I'd never say to his face but had grappled with over and over in prayer: "I forgive you, Dad. Goodbye."

I took one last look at him, and that was the last time I saw my dad alive.

"Be at peace," I said quietly once Bill and I were back in the car and heading home.

Seven months later on a Saturday morning, my dad died peacefully, his body finally giving out. But it was that day in the hospital when the anger left me completely. In forgiving him, I set myself free.

epilogue

Present day

Now, here I am on the other side of all that trauma. While I'm still healing, I've come many miles from where I was. I no longer struggle with suicidal thoughts or the depression I once suffered with. I've learned to love myself and allow myself to feel all my emotions without judgment.

My healing came slowly and is still coming. It took being honest with myself and others about what I really thought about things. Believe me, that was scary but so worth it. Finding a good counselor and sticking with it was huge for me. Even in that, I had to be completely honest with what I struggled with and had to determine to change how I thought about things and, more importantly, myself.

Some of my family have not been comfortable with me speaking about my truth, so I've tried my hardest to shield them as much as possible while still maintaining honesty. The biggest thing that changed me was understanding who I was to God. I wasn't a second-rate kid of his; I was his full daughter, endowed with all the things that a daughter is entitled to. And so are you! It's vital to completely understand who you really are and begin to change how you think about yourself—to see yourself as God sees you.

I hope my story will inspire you not to give up on God and what he can do in you. With him, seemingly insurmountable wounds can be healed.

And it can be a beautiful healing.

acknowledgments

To God. There aren't enough words or thoughts I could put on this paper that would begin to be adequate to thank you, praise you, and acknowledge you. Nevertheless, this is your story and your victory. Thank you for letting me tell it and for keeping me through things I thought I wouldn't survive. I love you!

Bill, without a doubt, you are the single most influential person in my life. Because of your shyness, most people do not get to see your wit and humor, which is a shame. I love laughing with you daily and am so grateful you loved me through some dark moments. God used you to heal so many deep hurts. You are the best man I have ever known, and I love you dearly.

Bertha, I know your prayers led me to know God. I miss you every day, and the world is darker without you.

Robert Noland, thank you for all your help and input and for putting up with a million questions. You've been the quasi-mentor to me to get this thing where it needs to be. I couldn't have done this without you.

Tiffany Brearton, I'm so thankful we are friends! You've encouraged me many times when I didn't think I could do any of this, and you listened to me implode and wrestle with this whole thing. Let's continue to bond over our love of God and alternative hair color!

Catherine KingsVail, my friend, my sister, my mentor. Words cannot express how much I love you and how much you have impacted me with your unfailing acceptance and advice. I am so glad I know you!!

Kelly Clark, thank you for our weekly calls. Your friendship has meant the world to me.

CST (Childhood Sexual Trauma) Group at Crossroads Church, I've been so honored to be a part of this group as a participant and leader. Thank you to all the experts who have been a part of speaking both into me and others. Those first steps to the recovery journey can be shaky, and this group helps guide people in ways that will impact generations to come.

Lorie Langdon, Carey Corp, and Melissa Landers, every girl needs friends like you! You guys bless me in so many ways. Thanks for being a sounding board over life and writing.

The Wednesday morning posse, Kelly Jewell, Rachel Cox and Rebeka Leinberger. I love you guys so much and appreciate all the times you heard me talk about this project over the many years it took to complete it. I love doing life with you guys through breakups, marriages, and births. You have the family you are born with and those you choose. I'm glad you have been part of my chosen family!

River of Life Church and the Woodard Family, thank you so much for the wonderful humans you are!

Lucretia Bowman, thank you for being a friend and a sister!

Lysa TerKeurst, for giving me that initial push to publish after hearing my story.

Billy, Kierdan, Kayleigh, Landon, and Aiden, you guys have my heart!

And to everyone else who I have failed to name here. There are many of you, and I want to say thank you to the remainder of my friends and family.

Last, but certainly not least, all my fur babies. I will not name you here, but I want to say you have helped me write this book by your constant presence.

about the author

Jennifer Osborn was raised in Southeastern Kentucky area. She was transplanted to the Cincinnati, Ohio area where she continues to live. Her writing has won various awards.

For speaking engagements: parableroadllc@gmail.com

www.jenniferosborn.org

facebook.com/AuthorJenniferOsborn
x.com/Jenosborn89
instagram.com/jenniferosborn_author

Made in the USA
Middletown, DE
30 December 2023

46385025R00096